C000318841

LETTS CREATIVE NEEDLECRAFTS

PATCHWORK

· JANE · WALMSLEY ·

LETTS CREATIVE NEEDLECRAFTS

PATCHWORK

JANE WALMSLEY

CHARLES LETTS · Letts · FOUNDED 1796

For John, Paula and Tim

First published 1990
by Charles Letts & Company Ltd
Diary House, Borough Road
London SE1 1DW

Reprinted in 1991

Designed and produced by Rosemary Wilkinson
30 Blackroot Road, Sutton Coldfield, B74 2QP

Illustrator: Richard Draper
Design coordinator: Patrick Knowles
Designer: Mike Spiller
Photographer: Daniel McGrath
Cover photograph: Pablo Keller

© Charles Letts & Company Ltd 1990

All our Rights Reserved. No part of this publication may be
reproduced, stored in a retrieval system, or transmitted, in any form or
by any means, electronic, mechanical, photocopying, recording or
otherwise, without the prior permission of Charles Letts Publishers.

'Letts' is a registered trademark of Charles Letts (Scotland) Ltd

CIP catalogue record for this book is available from the British Library

ISBN 1 85238 107 8

Typeset by Fakenham Photosetting Ltd, Fakenham, Norfolk

Printed in Belgium

CONTENTS

Design: Past and present   10
Starter Pack   14
Skill File   16
Rigid Star   22
Baby Ball   26
Christmas Wreath   30
Scalloped Christmas Wreath   34
Advent Calendar   38
Christmas Stocking   42
Polescreen   46
Build a Quilt   50
Log Cabin   64
Double Wedding Ring Throw   70
Seminole and Strip Patchwork   76
Basket of Grapes   82
Skill File: Quilting and finishing   88
Care and Conservation   91
Glossary   92
Index   93

Close-up of an Album quilt from New Jersey, U.S.A., presented to the Rev. Mrs Waterbury on April 1, 1853

DESIGN: PAST AND PRESENT

The changing styles and uses of patchwork around the world from intricate friendship quilts to warm and homely bedlinen

Patchwork and appliqué can be viewed as economy forms of needlework: at the most basic level, cutting sound pieces of fabric from otherwise worn textiles and scraps, then resewing them into bed covers, hangings, clothes, etc., or applying a patch over a worn area of cloth. However as man is inherently creative: the applied patch was shaped and possibly embellished with stitching and the pieced patches were organized into patterns and colours.

Historically, patchwork, appliqué and quilting have been known in many countries, including India, Pakistan, Sudan, the Middle East, Europe and later America, Canada and Australia. Little evidence of early pieces survive, although there are occasional references in literature and in the lists of household inventories. In a remote part of India, which was on the old silk route from Europe to China, a discovery was made, in a walled up chapel, of patchwork made from small pieces of silk left by travellers, oversewn together on the back probably by a priest. In the Boulak Museum in Cairo there is a gazelle hide appliqué canopy dating from about 980 B.C. The symbols that appear on it can be seen on today's cotton appliqué.

Crusader banners and other heraldic devices used patchwork and appliqué as do banners to the present day.

Appliqué was often combined with embroidery and was used for ecclesiastical as well as house furnishings. In Hardwick Hall, England, there are wall hangings made by Bess of Hardwick which incorporate beautiful and rare fabrics.

In Britain patchwork, appliqué and quilting are linked, and all three crafts can be used separately or together in one article. Quilting serves to anchor the top, wadding and backing fabrics, as well as being decorative. However, patchwork and appliqué are often not quilted. Patchwork can also be simply an economical way of making a backing for the quilt.

The introduction of the painted calico and chintz cotton palampores and bed hangings to Europe from India in the 17th century led to sophisticated bed covers and hangings being made in appliqué. The printed designs were cut out and stitched onto a plain background fabric. Many of these bed furnishings were beautiful, made by women with access to the luxury fabrics and with time to spend on both exquisite sewing and design. Geometric patchwork and combinations of appliqué and patchwork were employed. The oldest known work using calicoes, dated 1708, is at Levens Hall.

Early in the 19th century special commemorative panels were printed and used for the centres of 'framed' quilts and coverlets. The centre panel would be surrounded by a succession of borders some of which may also have been specially printed, others made of patchwork or strips of printed fabrics. One such panel celebrated George III's Golden Jubilee in 1810. Other popular fabrics of the time were the Game Birds prints.

By 1830 cotton fabrics with small scale printed designs were both cheap and readily available and were used in pieced patchwork.

In the middle of the 19th century, crazy patchwork was in vogue, made from irregular patches of silks, satins and velvets laid on a foundation fabric, their overlapping raw edges decorated with feather stitch worked in yellow thread through all layers. More elaborate crazy patchwork was made using the same mix of fabrics, but the edges and patches were extensively embroidered and beaded, almost smothering the fabrics. These were used as table covers, sofa throws, and even slippers.

Mosaic patchwork, made from various geometric shapes, such as hexagons, diamonds, triangles, squares and octagons tacked over papers, then oversewn on the wrong side, also used silks, satins and velvets. This was a very popular form of patchwork, some totally random others beautifully planned and executed. Even when the patchwork has not been used, the silk has often rotted due to the

A 20th century Hawaiian quilt in red and white

'weighting' of inferior silk fabrics for then fashionable large puff sleeves and crinoline skirts. Mosaic work was also made cheaply and economically in cotton fabrics but was not favoured by the fashionable. However, of the patchwork which survives from this period, the cotton examples have stood the test of time far better.

Hospital quilts made from red and white cotton squares in a chequerboard pattern, with pictures and tracts from the scriptures written on them, were said to be very popular with the patients.

Patchwork, appliqué and quilting were taken to North America by settlers from

Europe. Although some patterns are held in common, a great variety of blocks (a single unit of patches) with evocative names have been created. When the requisite number of blocks was made they were stitched together in many different ways to make the patchwork top. A sandwich of top, wadding and backing was then quilted together making very warm, attractive bed covers. Families needed many quilts to keep them warm, so some would be very homely, possibly with tied quilting, with the more carefully designed and executed quilt being kept for the top cover.

Album or Friendship quilts would be made by a community to give to a departing church minister or friend. In this case each block would be made by a different person, and the group would come together to quilt it. These much-prized quilts were often never used, so many survive for our enjoyment today.

The Amish community has contributed to the American piecework tradition in a very positive way. A Christian sect, the Amish originally fled from Switzerland via Germany to escape religious persecution, to live in farming communities, eschewing modern machinery. The Amish made stunning quilts, mainly using large geometric shapes, in strong, plain vibrant colours with exquisite workmanship in the construction and quilting.

Seminole Indians of Florida have a unique method of making patchwork. Strips of fabric are machine sewn together, making a whole textile, which is cut again into strips, some straight, some angled. These are then resewn into intricate patchwork strips which are particularly applicable to clothing.

The missionaries introduced needlework to Hawaii, and the result is yet another individual interpretation. The designs are created by the folded and cut paper technique, but in this case the design is large enough to cover the whole quilt top. Only two colours are used, often red with white. One colour is applied to the other, then the whole is quilted following the contours of the design.

In the early 19th century, Elizabeth Fry, the Quaker prison reformer, used patchwork as one way of helping women in Newgate Prison, London. Prisoners might be sentenced to transportation to Van Diemens Land. During this terrifying voyage some of the women carried on with their patchwork using fabrics given to them by the Female Prison Reform Association. Some sold the quilts on arrival, others kept them. In Australia aboriginal women were the first to make patchwork for clothes and bedlinen.

The idea of patchwork as therapy also extended to soldiers in hospital; there is a famous painting of Private Walker in a hospital bed making patchwork from soldiers' uniforms. At this time uniform fabric was thick, woven wool, which felted and therefore did not fray. Colours included red, yellow, brown and black; the designs were simple but strong.

Patchwork, appliqué and quilting have been enjoying a renaissance during the past few years with a great cross fertilization of ideas, designs and enthusiasms between all who are interested.

FABRICS

Fabrics made from natural fibres, e.g. cotton, silk and wool, are ideal for various forms of patchwork. It is generally advisable to use the same weight fabric in any one project.

Cotton   Cotton wears and launders well, is easy to handle and is available in quite a wide range of weights, weaves, prints and plains. Closely-woven dress weight fabrics work very well. Lightweight furnishing cotton, as long as it is woven from good quality fine yarns can be used, but sometimes the designs are too big and sparse for patchwork. Wash cotton fabrics and remove selvages before use.

Polyester-cotton blends   These blends with not more than 50% polyester can be used but they tend to be springy and can stretch, so they do not fold well or press flat in seams, etc. They can also be very thin.

Silk   Silk is a luxury fabric, not as robust as cotton, and should be dry cleaned. It is available in a delicious variety of printed and plain fabrics. Use a good quality silk – some are too thin; and do not use crêpe-like weaves, as they will not cut into sharp, stable patches.

Wool   Wool comes in various weights, colours and weaves, the finer of which make up into rich-looking patchwork, usually in the simpler designs, with larger patches.

Tweeds, suitings and heavier weight fabrics have been used by patchworkers both in the past and the present day to very good effect. Should be dry cleaned.

WADDING

If the article is to be quilted, various choices are available:

Polyester wadding   In various weights, 2 oz, 3 oz, 4 oz, and some even thicker. For fine quilting 2 oz wadding works well, polyester wadding is widely available, lightweight, washes well and is very good for both beginners and more experienced patchworkers.

Silk wadding   Available in various weights. It is available by the yard and has a slightly stiff papery surface on both sides. Spun silk fibres sandwiched between very fine silk fabric is also available.

Cotton wadding   By the yard with slightly stiff papery surfaces.

Classic wadding   80% cotton, 20% polyester, available by the piece from some patchwork suppliers.

Cotton domette and wool domette   Available from some fabric shops, will give a flattish effect, useful for clothes where high loft is not desired.

Acrilan wadding   Longish fibres between papery top and bottom layers. Again, a flattish effect but also a little stiff.

Carded sheep's wool   Was used in the past particularly in Welsh quilts. To stop the fibres migrating through the quilt top and backing, the sheep's wool can be first enclosed in butter muslin.

Woollen blankets   Were used in the past, these would give a fairly flat finish to the quilting and would be quite heavy.

NEEDLES FOR HAND SEWING

The finer the needle, the finer the stitches you can sew. Generally sizes 9 and 10 are used in the following types:

Betweens   A short needle with a small eye, used for fine sewing and quilting.

Sharps   A slightly longer needle with a small eye, used for general sewing and tacking.

Crewel   The same length as the Sharps, but with a larger eye. Truly an embroidery needle but can be used for general sewing and tacking.

NEEDLES FOR MACHINE SEWING

Ensure that the needle is sharp and the correct size for the textile being stitched as stipulated in the manufacturer's handbook.

PINS

You will need plenty of good quality rustless pins. Fine and extra long or glass headed. Also, have a separate tin or box for the pins, not one with a mixture of paper clips, elastic bands, drawing pins, etc. *Please*, just pins for sewing!

SCISSORS

Three pairs are needed: good quality dressmaking scissors for cutting fabric; small, sharp, embroidery scissors; scissors to cut paper and curved edges on templates.

Do not cut paper, etc., with fabric scissors, as it will blunt them.

SEWING THREAD

Use a fine cotton thread for cotton and woollen fabrics and silk thread for silk fabric, usually in a neutral tone to blend into the work, but it may be necessary to use more than one colour – experiment!

TEMPLATES

Some commercial templates are available. Learn to make your own, it is much more rewarding.

Thick card   Readily available and makes good templates (do not use old cereal packets, these are often waxed and not substantial enough).

Plastic sheet   Available from some patchwork suppliers; is almost ideal – it is translucent, which means the design can be traced leaving the original intact, it cuts accurately with a Stanley knife (heavyweight craft knife) or scissors for curves. Be careful, though, being translucent it can be 'lost' and do not iron it!

Medium weight sandpaper   Can be used for templates for smaller projects.

Strip templates   Available from some patchwork suppliers, they come in a variety of widths and are useful for strip patchwork.

PAPERS

Papers for patchwork   When making patchwork by tacking fabric onto papers, use a crisp paper, such as cartridge, new, good quality brown paper or old, glossy magazines. The papers for this form of patchwork need to be firm enough to allow you to feel the edge when turning the seam allowance over, but flexible enough to fold when sewing patches together.

Graph paper   For planning projects and drafting blocks and templates. Isometric graph paper is used for hexagons, etc.

Drawing paper   For drafting 8 pointed star blocks, etc.

OTHER EQUIPMENT

Thimble   If you do not use a thimble, try to learn to; it will be especially helpful when quilting.

Pencils   Hard pencils in 2H or 4H for drawing templates and plans. Coloured pencils for marking fabrics; keep them sharp.

Sandpaper   1 large sheet of new sandpaper (or several sheets taped together) are used to stop fabric slipping while marking around templates.

Ruler   A 30 cm (12 in) metal ruler for use with a Stanley knife (heavyweight craft knife) when cutting templates.

A ruler, protractor, compass and set square for drafting blocks and templates.

Rotary cutter and cutting mat   These must be used in conjunction with one another. They are excellent for cutting fabric strips, borders, etc. The cutting mat is 'self healing', so the surface remains smooth. They are quite expensive pieces of equipment but are extremely useful.

Sewing Machine   For patchwork the machine only needs to be able to sew in a straight line, but needs to be kept in good order to ensure that the thread tension is correct.

30 cm (12 in) cork or polystyrene tile   Mounted on thick card or hardboard and covered with calico or any plain cotton fabric. Pin the cut fabric shapes in sequence on this board; this ensures that the correct shapes are sewn together.

Beeswax   Beeswax is used to coat the sewing thread when hand sewing. It helps to stop tangling and wear on thread. It is a useful aid to quilting too. *N.B. When hand sewing do not have the thread longer than 45 cm (18 in).*

COLOUR SCHEME AND FABRICS

Patchwork depends upon shape and colour for its impact. Usually one has a colour scheme in mind around which to build the design. Within this chosen scheme contrasts between *light, medium and dark tones* are necessary to delineate the patchwork patterns.

Within the colour scheme add an 'accent' colour in small amounts; this is usually a contrasting colour, the addition of which will make the patchwork lively.

If the colour scheme is a 'cold' one, i.e. blues or greens, introduce a small amount of a 'hot' colour: red, yellow, orange, pink – and vice versa with a mainly 'hot' scheme.

All plain fabrics will give a sharply-defined design (see the Roman Stripe and the Log Cabin quilts on pages 78 and 66). Many historic quilts made in just two colours of turkey red and white or blue and white are very striking (see the Hawaiian quilt, page 12).

If only patterned fabrics are used the finished article could look very 'busy', some areas of rest are required.

When using a mixture of printed and plain fabrics, vary the size of the prints, some small, some medium and some large. Centring the fabric design within a patchwork shape or using striped fabrics can create interest and variety. Look at the two Castle Wall blocks in the sampler quilt (page 62), although made from the same shapes, varying the position of the fabrics creates a very different effect.

CHOOSING THE FABRIC

The choice of fabric fibre to be used is a wide one (see also page 14). However, if the article is to be in constant use it will need to be washable; 100% dress weight cotton fabric will work well. It has the added advantages of being easy to sew and 'doing what it's told'. It is the best choice for a beginner, too. Polycotton mixture fabrics come in a tantalizingly wide range of colours, but I have found that they tend to stretch and do not always lie flat, so prefer not to use them.

Silk is a delight to work with, but it is a delicate fabric. The colour range is enormous, translucent and very exciting, but see page 14 for silks to avoid.

Wool is also a lovely fabric to use, both in light dress weights and the heavier suitings and tweeds.

Collecting the fabrics for any patchwork project can be a lengthy process, but be patient at this crucial early stage.

As pieces of fabric are bought, cut a length from each piece about 2.5 × 7.5 cm (1 × 3 in) and staple one end of each fabric on to a piece of paper, then you can lay the free end of the samples on fabrics before purchasing them to ascertain whether they fit into your colour scheme. A small square of fabric stuck on to a white piece of paper gives an incorrect reading as the white (or whatever colour the paper is) moderates the colour of the sample. Generally a minimum of 6 different fabrics would be required for larger projects.

When these fabrics have been collected, fold them in rectangles of about 25 × 15 cm (10 × 6 in) and lay them out in a fan shape (diagram 1). In this way you can check how the

colours are reacting upon one another in small amounts at the base of the fan and in larger areas at the top. Change the sequence and check again to ensure that you have an interesting and pleasurable colour scheme. Also look at them through half closed eyes, this enables the tonal value to show and will help you plan the positions of the different fabrics.

WASHING THE COTTON FABRICS

Take your pile of smooth, pristine cotton fabrics and wash them – this hurts! However, it is necessary, since washing shrinks the fabric. (Warp and weft threads can shrink at different rates, think about an unwashed square of fabric, washed it could became a rectangle, now think of a patchwork quilt made entirely of unwashed fabrics, the first time it is laundered . . .!) Washing will also test for colourfastness and remove any dressing. Iron the fabrics carefully ensuring the threads are straight.

N.B. Fabric suppliers usually specify that fabrics should be washed at low temperature and that biological powders should not be used.

This obviously does not apply to fabrics which are 'dry clean only'.

THE DESIGN PLAN

There are various different types of patchwork, each of which requires a different design approach.

Block designs

Having chosen the patchwork design from the many available (see North American Blocks section for some possibilities) make a scale plan of the complete article.

Experiment with the methods of assembly: should the blocks be sewn directly next to one another? For Log Cabin, the answer is yes: whether the diagonal light and dark or courthouse steps arrangement has been used, the interest lies in the pattern created when the blocks are placed directly next to each other

(see page 69). For other blocks there are many possibilities: sashing, alternating with plain squares, setting the blocks square, setting the blocks on point, making a central panel and surrounding this with borders, etc. (see pages 54 and 55).

Graph paper can be used to plan many of the designs, but isometric graph paper will be required for hexagons, etc.

Hexagon based designs

Looking at the various designs shown in diagrams 2 to 4, the relationship between hexagons, 60° diamonds and equilateral triangles can readily be seen, as can the

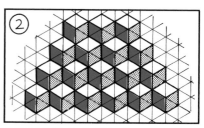

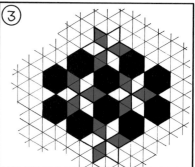

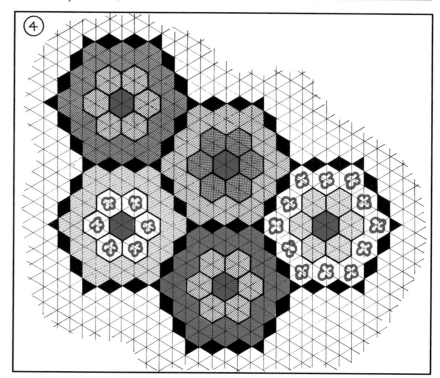

almost limitless design variations which are possible through the interlinking of these three shapes. Experiment, doodle with a pencil, it can be very exciting.

Curved seam patchwork

One of the best known curved designs is Double Wedding Ring (page 70) consisting of interlocking circles rather than square blocks.

8 Pointed Star based designs

With their long diamonds, these shapes will not fit graph paper grids, so when planning the design, draw the basic block on to plain paper and either take multiple tracings or photocopy, then cut the blocks out, assemble them in the required pattern and glue in position (see page 53 for two block designs).

Crazy patchwork

Crazy patchwork was very popular in the 19th century. Here, mixed fabrics such as silks, satins, ribbons and velvet were all used in the same article. Fabric scraps in random shapes were placed on a backing fabric, with raw edges overlapping, the edges were then stitched down with embroidery through all the layers. Feather stitch was used in the simpler ones with very elaborate embroidery in the more ornate examples. No plan or template is needed for this patchwork.

Appliqué

In this form of patchwork, shapes are applied to a background fabric which is part of the design.

Appliqué designs can be very stylized as in some American block patterns. These designs will be quilted, so after each shape is applied, the backing fabric is carefully cut away just leaving 6 mm (¼ in) seam allowances. This is then used as a guide for the quilting lines.

When a more realistic design is required, many more small pieces are used to build up the form. In this case the actual 'building up' becomes part of the design, giving texture, as in the Basket of Grapes Appliqué Picture (page 82), which is not quilted and therefore the backing fabric is left intact.

Drafting the full size block

Having drawn the plan add the full size measurements, so that the actual size of the component blocks can be calculated. Draft one of these complete blocks to the actual size by first drawing the exact size of the outer square i.e. the unit of design without seam allowances. If

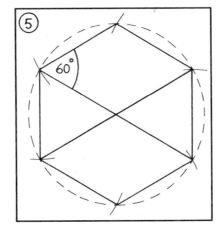

appropriate, draw the grid within this square, then draw in all the pattern lines using a ruler and 2H or 4H pencil sharpened to a fine point. It is absolutely essential that all lines are drawn accurately, as it is from this block that the templates will be made (see the design sheet, page 53). Seam allowances will be added when marking the fabric. The number and shape of the templates which make up the block will now been seen.

To draw templates for hexagons, etc. Using a compass, set the radius to the desired length of one side of the hexagon. Draw a circle, then still with the same radius draw 6 arcs bisecting the circle setting the point of the compass on the preceding arc. Connect the points where the arcs cross the circle, thus outlining the hexagon. If lines are drawn across the hexagon, as shown in diagram 5, the 60° diamond and equilateral triangle which are compatible with the hexagon will appear.

Templates can be made from medium weight card, sandpaper (where the use of the template will be limited), metal* or transparent plastic sheet. The preferred method of cutting is with a Stanley knife (fitted with a new, sharp retractable blade).

* Commercial templates, which have a limited size and pattern range are frequently made from metal and often come with a window template for use when marking fabric.

TO MAKE THE TEMPLATES

A specially-made plastic is available (page 15). It is easy to use as it is translucent, can be laid on the drafted design, and the shape traced on, leaving the original draft intact. Each template must have all its lines drawn individually, using a 2H pencil, to ensure accuracy.

If card is to be used either take a careful tracing or draw a replica template shape on graph paper. Glue these on to the card (or smooth side of the sandpaper) with a glue-stick and cut with the heavyweight craft knife. It is advisable to keep the original design in case templates are lost or damaged. It is also prudent to cut several sets of card templates if a large project is to be undertaken as they become worn and inaccurate in use.

CUTTING THE TEMPLATES

Lay the drawn templates on a cutting board (can be thick card or hardboard, to protect surfaces). Place the metal ruler exactly along a marked line with the ruler on the template area, make an accurate and careful cut against the ruler, scoring the surface, then keep running the knife along the ruler until the template is cut through (diagram 6). Scissors can be used for curved lines.

This is a *finished size template*.

WINDOW TEMPLATES

Window templates can also be cut from card or sandpaper, mark as for template, but draw an additional line 6 mm (¼ in) away from finished size template. Cut the centre section out carefully and also cut on outer line (diagram 7a). This will enable a

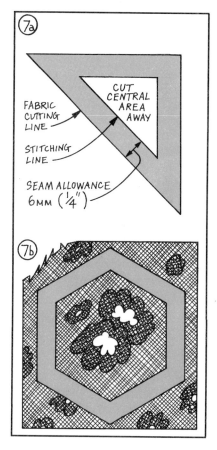

motif in the fabric to be centred within the template shape (diagram 7b). If plastic has been used it is not necessary to make a window template as an outline of the particular part of the design can be drawn on to the plastic in the appropriate position.

CUTTING THE FABRICS

Before using fabric cut selvages off, as they can be made from inferior yarns and will make a hard ridge under the patchwork. Smooth the

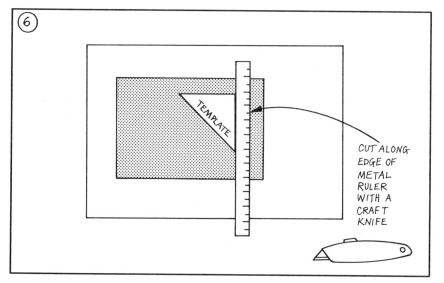

fabric, right side down, on to a sheet of fine sandpaper. This will hold the fabric while marking. Place the template so that at least one edge is on the grain of the fabric (i.e. parallel to the selvage). Draw around the template on the wrong side of the fabric with a well sharpened pencil: this marked line will be the *stitching line* also referred to as the seam line. *Add 6 mm (¼ in) all around each shape,* this will give the cutting line (diagram 8). A blunt pencil will give an inaccurate shape – keep it sharp! Cut the fabric carefully, along the cutting line using sharp scissors.

N.B. Templates given in the book are marked with an arrow to show the direction of the grain where this is important.

Mark and cut all the necessary pieces for the block. Pin onto a thick cork or polystyrene tile (page 15) in their correct sequence.

METHOD OF CONSTRUCTION

Work out the stitching sequence, wherever possible straight lines make easier sewing.

Decide whether the article is to be hand or machine sewn. Many of the more complicated designs, where angles have to be set in, or long points matched, are perhaps better achieved by hand sewing.

1. Seamed patchwork sometimes referred to as the American method.

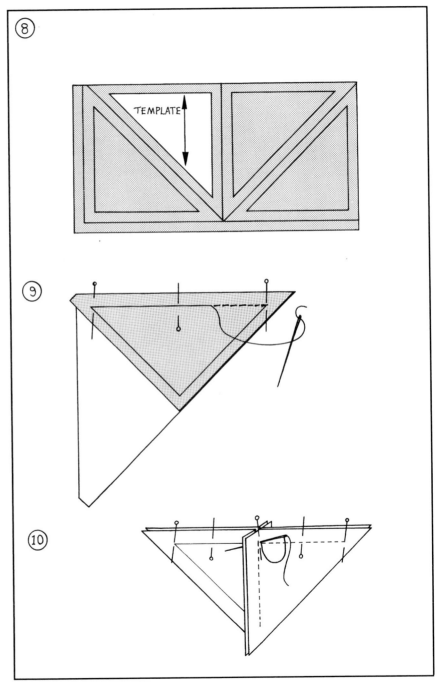

Place 2 patches right sides together, match corner points and place pins at right angles to stitching line, place another pin in centre. Starting and finishing with secure back stitches, sew patches together with small, even running stitches strengthened with an occasional back stitch, *along marked seam line only* not into seam allowances (diagram 9). Carefully press seam allowances both the same way, wherever possible on to the darker fabric.

When stitching groups of patches together it will be necessary to cross seam lines. Pin as before, carefully matching seam lines, stitch up to the seam line, make a back stitch, pass needle through seam allowance, make another back stitch and continue to end of marked line (diagram 10). This ensures that the points will meet exactly.

Continue in this manner, stitching units together until block is completed.

Construct all the blocks in the same way.

2. Hand sewing using papers also called the English method; particularly useful for mosaic patchwork (i.e. hexagons, etc.).

Make templates as detailed previously, then draw around template on crisp paper and cut accurately on marked line. Pin paper shapes to wrong side of fabric and cut fabric with added 6 mm (1/4 in) seam allowances all round

shape (diagram 11a). Fold seam allowance over paper and tack in position (diagram 11b). Make up sufficient shapes in this manner to make a unit. Place two shapes, right sides together, carefully oversew together along one side picking up only the edge of the folded fabric. Open out, place the next shape in position and so on until motif is finished (diagram 11c). The papers should stay in the item until it is completed, then remove the tacking threads and lift papers out.

3. Construction by sewing machine. Some of the simpler block shapes can be sewn by machine, again using the seamed method of construction. Log Cabin lends itself readily to the sewing machine (see page 65 where details are given for preparation for machine sewing).

Seminole and Strip Patchwork, which are both sewn and recut, must be machine stitched together. See pages 76 to 81 for cutting and sewing techniques.

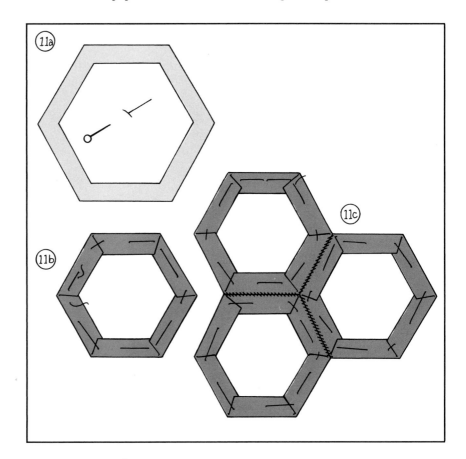

RIGID STAR

This highly decorative star is based on the 'English' method of patchwork, but the card shapes are left in place, as they are an integral part of the construction. It consists of twelve 'flowers' made from six different coloured silks and is assembled in such a way that different colours are adjacent to one another. The star could, perhaps, be considered a challenge.

REQUIREMENTS

Pieces of silk in 6 different colours, each 25 × 20 cm (10 × 8 in), to make 12 'flowers' each constructed from 5 diamonds
Packet of plain postcards
Packet of 14 mm (⅝ in) long pins
32 pearl beads
Packet of small glass beads

CUTTING DETAILS

Cut 60 diamond shapes from the postcards, using the diamond template, i.e. enough for 12 'flowers' made up of 5 'petals' each. In this rigid form of patchwork the card shapes remain in the work.
Mark and cut the fabric, adding 6 mm (¼ in) seam allowance all round, in two sets of five from each colour.

Fold the fabric over the card shapes, do not tack through the card, but back stitch through the pleat made on each corner, ensure that the folds are sharply creased before turning

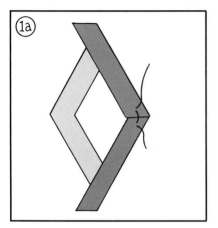

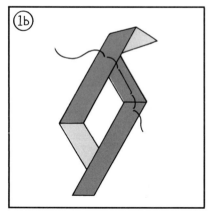

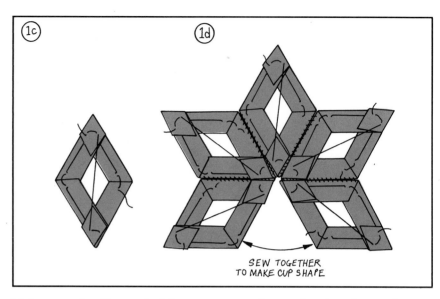

SEW TOGETHER
TO MAKE CUP SHAPE

the corner (diagrams 1a and 1b). Do not trim the excess fabric but turn the 'tails', which are formed on the sharp points, back on to the seam allowance and back stitch (diagram 1c). There should be a little 'give' on each shape to enable them to be sewn together without tearing the fabric.

Make up twelve 'flowers' of five diamonds each by oversewing the diamonds together on the wrong side. This will give a cup shape (diagram 1d). Stitch a pearl bead in the centre.

Stitch six 'flowers' together on the right side using ladder stitch (page 92) thus:

Place flower 1 against flower 2 matching points A and C and seams B and B. Stitch in position, then place flower 3 against 1, again matching and stitching C, B, A. Next match and stitch flowers 2 and 3, matching C, B, A (diagram 2). Note that at C, three diamonds form a point. Continue adding flowers 4, 5 and 6 around the central flower 1. This completes half the star. Make the other half in the same manner.

Before stitching the two halves

together, make a hanging cord or ribbon, tying a large knot which will be sewn inside the star. Attach the cord between a seam B (diagram 2) rather than at a point C. Ladder stitch the two halves together to complete the star.

Slip a small bead on to a short pin and push through an external seam. Repeat until all the outer seams are covered. A larger pearl bead on each point adds character (diagram 3).

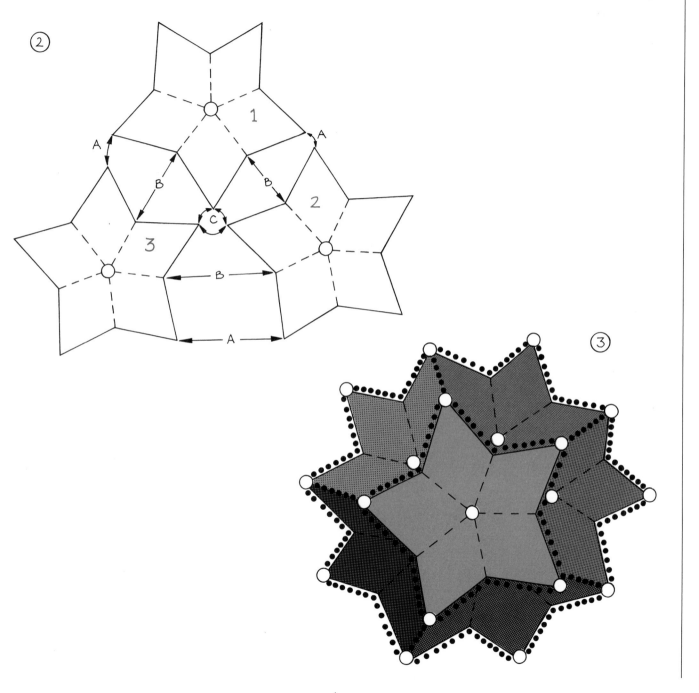

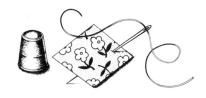

BABY BALL

A ball formed from twelve segments. The bright colours are especially attractive to babies and they will find the wedge shapes easy to grasp. The cotton fabrics and stuffing will launder well in the washing machine. Made in Christmas colours, the same ball would make a delightful festive decoration.

CONSTRUCTION

REQUIREMENTS

25 cm (¼ yard) cotton fabric, colour A
25 cm (¼ yard) cotton fabric, colour B
25 cm (¼ yard) cotton fabric, colour C
Bag of non-flammable toy stuffing

CUTTING DETAILS

Use the template diagrams on page 29, adding 6 mm (¼ in) seam allowances all round each shape.
Template 1: 12 in colour A
Template 1: 12 in colour B
Template 2: 12 in colour C

N.B. These shapes must be machine or back stitched on all seams. The stitching needs to be strong enough to enable the wedges to be stuffed firmly.

Place the curved edge of shape 1, colour A, on the curved edge of shape 2, right sides together, matching centres. Stitch along the marked line, *not into the seam allowance* (diagram 1a).

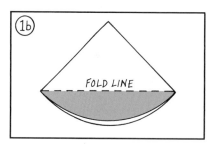

Fold shape 2 in half (diagram 1b).

Place the second shape 1, colour B, right sides together over the pieces

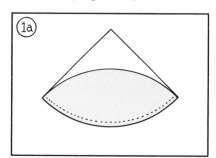

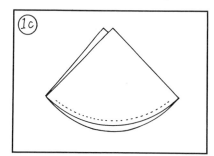

already stitched. The curved edge will then match the second edge of shape 2 which has been folded over. Stitch along the marked lines on curves only, matching centres (diagram 1c).

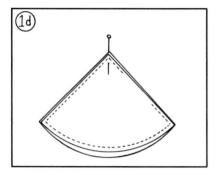

Pin the points of shapes 1 together. Stitch along the marked lines on the straight edges, leaving an opening as shown in diagram 1d. Turn the wedge shape right side out. Stuff the wedge firmly, then stitch the openings together.

Make eleven more wedges in the same way.

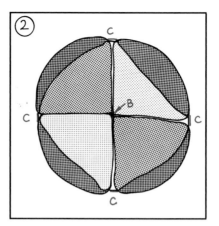

Oversew four segments together *securely* at points B and C, using double thread (diagram 2).

Stitch two pairs of segments together at points D and B, then attach these together at point E (diagram 3).

Place the set of segments just made over the four stitched together previously, so that they are at right angles to each other. Stitch together at point F. Also secure them at the centre (diagram 4).

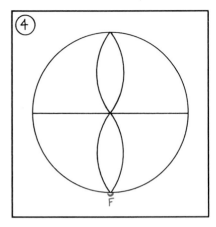

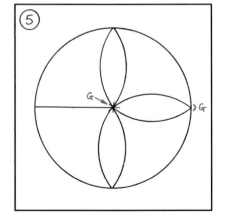

Insert the remaining four wedges individually and horizontally across the middle, pushing their points into the centre (it will not be possible to stitch them at the centre). Attach securely at each end of the wedge, i.e. at point G (diagram 5).

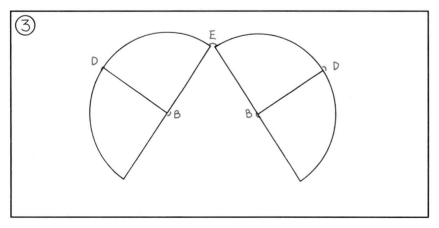

A hanging ribbon can be added if making a Christmas ball *but do not add to a baby ball as this could be hazardous.*

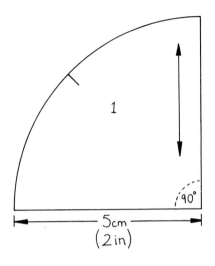

1

90°

5cm
(2 in)

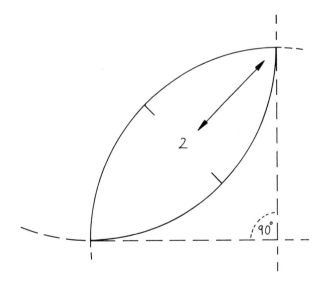

2

90°

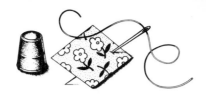

CHRISTMAS WREATH

This and the design which follows can be simply
made utilizing the many colourful, exciting and decorative
fabrics available, adding a personal touch to the
traditional family Christmas decorations.

REQUIREMENTS

50 cm (½ yard) fabric A
25 cm (¼ yard) fabric B
50 cm (½ yard) wadding
  (any weight)
4 metres (4 yards) narrow
  ribbon
Bag of non-flammable toy
  stuffing

CUTTING DETAILS

Use the template diagrams
  on page 33, adding 6 mm
  (¼ in) seam allowance
  around all shapes. See
  below for instructions on
  making template 1.
Template 1: 1 in colour A
Template 1: 2 in wadding
Template 2: 4 in colour A
Template 2: 4 in colour B
Template 3: 4 in colour A
Template 3: 4 in colour B

CONSTRUCTION

To make template 1 for the back of
the wreath, fold a 40 cm (16 in)
square of tracing paper into
quarters. Line up the fold lines with
the dotted lines on the quarter
template and mark the curved lines.
Cut while still folded, this will give
a complete template (diagram 1).
Attach the complete template to a
piece of thin card with a little glue
stick and cut out the card.

Join the outer edge of the smaller
arc (template 2) in colour A to the
inner edge of the larger arc
(template 3) in colour B, matching
notches and using the seamed
method (page 20) by hand or
machine, then join the small arc in
colour B to the large arc in colour A
(diagram 2). Complete three more
arcs in each colour combination in
the same way.

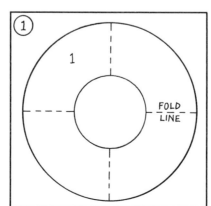

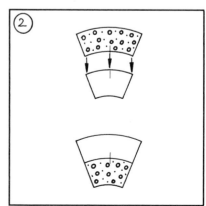

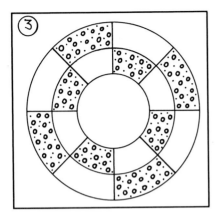

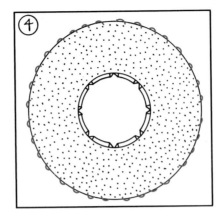

Join the eight sections together, alternating the colours (taking care to match the seam lines); this will make the complete wreath front (diagram 3).

Stay stitch the inner edge on both front and back of the wreath (i.e. template 1, colour A).

Place the back and front of the wreath right sides together and stitch around the outer edge along the marked line.

Loosely slip stitch the wadding circles on the front and back around the outer edge (diagram 4), then turn through to the right side.

Stuff with toy filling, to give a pleasing plumpness between the layers of wadding.

Snip the centre seam allowances almost to stay stitching lines, roll allowance and stay stitching to the wrong side, then tack in position on both back and front of the wreath. Bring back and front together, pin and stab stitch with small even stitches all round the centre (diagram 5). Remove the tacking stitches.

Cut the ribbon into eight equal lengths, pass the ribbon around the wreath over the seam lines, squeeze the wreath a little and tie the ribbon in a knot, then tie a bow with the excess ribbon (diagram 6). Finish with trim as desired and make a small hanging loop at the top.

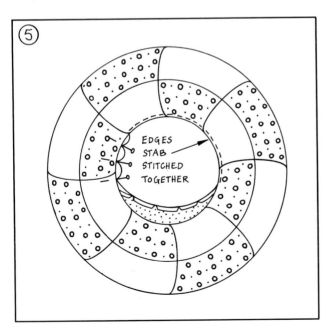

TEMPLATES

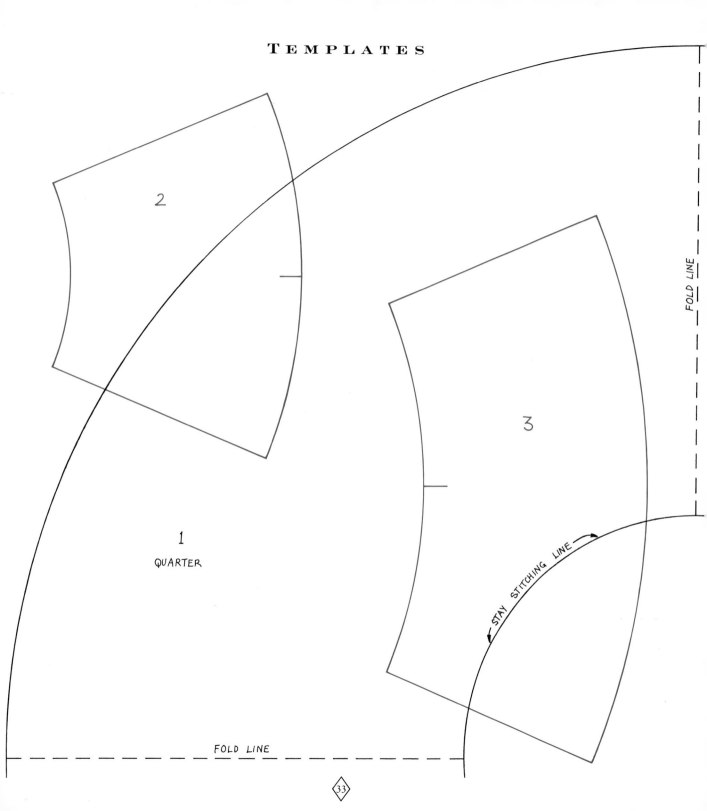

2

1

QUARTER

3

FOLD LINE

STAY STITCHING LINE

FOLD LINE

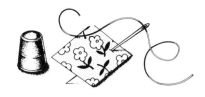

SCALLOPED CHRISTMAS WREATH

A further idea for a long-lasting fabric wreath. The construction is broadly similar, though a decorative frill is included in this design.

REQUIREMENTS

50 cm (½ yard) fabric, colour A
25 cm (¼ yard) fabric, colour B
25 cm (¼ yard) fabric, colour C for frill
50 cm (½ yard) polyester wadding (any weight)
Bag of non-flammable toy stuffing

CUTTING DETAILS

Use the template diagrams on page 37. N.B. For this item add 1 cm (½ in) seam allowance on all fabric shapes. See below for instructions on making template 1.
Template 1: 1 in colour A
Template 1: 2 in wadding
Template 2: 4 in colour A
Template 2: 4 in colour B

CONSTRUCTION

To make template 1 for the back of the wreath, fold a 40 cm (16 in) square of tracing paper into quarters. Line up the fold lines with the dotted lines on the quarter template and mark the curved lines. Cut while still folded, this will give a complete template (diagram 1). Attach the complete template to a piece of thin card with a little glue stick and cut out the card.

Place scallop shapes (template 2), colours A and B, right sides together in pairs, stitch along one straight edge on marked line only by hand or machine (diagram 2).

Stitch the pairs together in fours, then stitch the halves thus made together, making the complete front

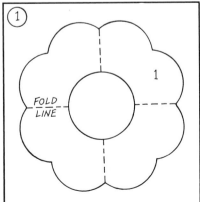

FOLD LINE

1

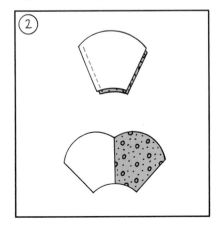

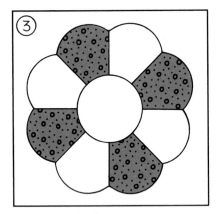

of the wreath (diagram 3).

Stay stitch the inner edge on both pieced front and the back of the wreath.

Make up a frill strip 200 × 10 cm (80 × 4 in) long (this measurement includes the seam allowance), piecing where necessary. Join into a continuous loop, fold in halves lengthwise, right sides out and press. Mark the quarters with pins. Stitch two lines of gathering threads, either by hand or machine, using a long stitch, the first row 6 mm (¼ in) in from the raw edges, then a parallel row 3 mm (⅛ in) in from the first line, stopping at each quarter pin (diagram 4). Further divide these sections in half, marking with pins, this will divide the frill into eight equal parts.

Pin the frill to the outer edge of the wreath front, matching the marker pins to the eight seam lines. Gently pull up the pairs of gathering threads until the frill fits the scalloped edges. Tack, then sew between the gathering threads (diagram 5).

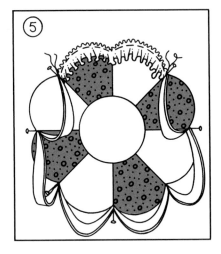

Lay the wreath back over the front, right sides together, matching the curved edges. Tack, then stitch in place securely.

Lay one wadding shape on the wrong side of the front and one on the wrong side of the back of the wreath. Loosely slip stitch to the outer raw edges. This helps to shape the scallops (diagram 6).

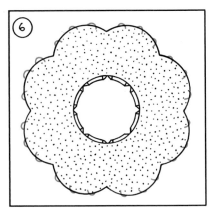

Turn to right side from the centre. Stuff with toy stuffing to give a pleasing plumpness between the layers of wadding.

Snip the centre seam allowances on front and back of wreath, almost to stay stitching lines. Roll allowance back over stitching, then tack. Bring back and front of wreath together, pin and stab stitch with small, even stitches (diagram 7). Remove the tacking. Finish the wreath as desired with ribbons, bows, bells, etc.

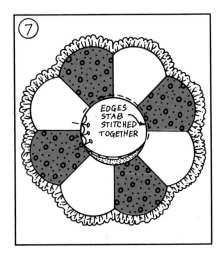

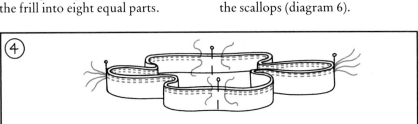

TEMPLATES

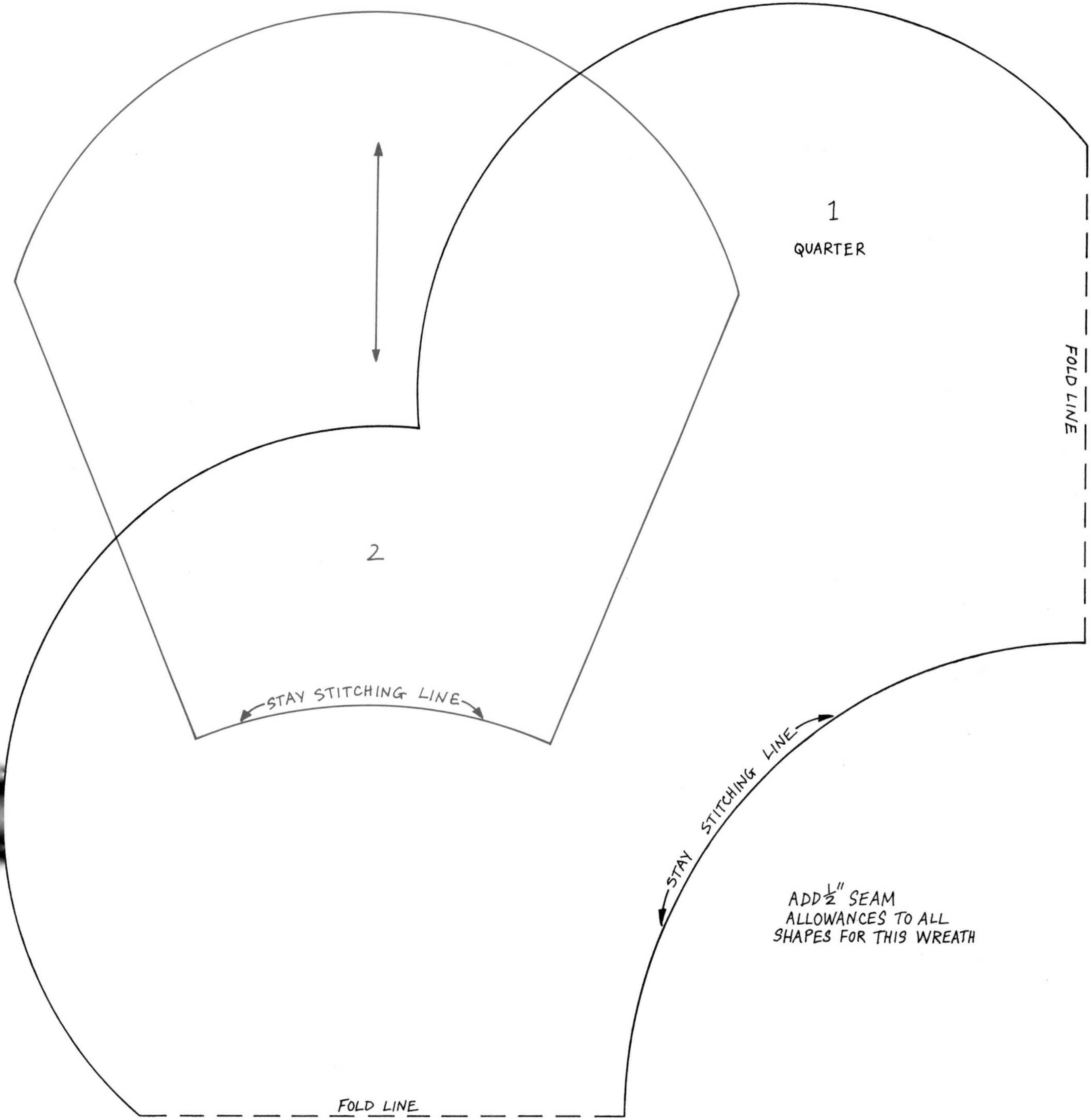

1

QUARTER

FOLD LINE

2

←STAY STITCHING LINE→

STAY STITCHING LINE

ADD $\frac{1}{2}$" SEAM
ALLOWANCES TO ALL
SHAPES FOR THIS WREATH

FOLD LINE

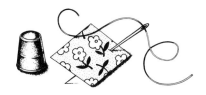

ADVENT CALENDAR

An original interpretation of the Advent Calendar
tradition. It is made from 25 diamonds, folded in half; the
triangles thus made hide 25 little pockets, which
can be filled with tiny gifts or chocolates to be discovered
day by day in the run up to Christmas.

50 cm (½ yard) cotton fabric,
colour A
30 cm (⅓ yard) cotton fabric,
colour B
30 cm (⅓ yard) cotton fabric,
colour C
25 × 10 cm (10 × 4 in) cotton
fabric for pot
15 × 8 cm (6 × 3 in) cotton fabric
for trunk
25 cm (¼ yard) lightweight iron-
on interlining
25 cm (¼ yard) 2 oz polyester
wadding
7 metres (7 yards) × 3 mm (⅛ in)
wide ribbon
1.5 metres (1½ yards) × 25 mm
(1 in) wide ribbon (must be at
least this wide to make the
'pockets')
21 small bells
6 press studs
Tapestry needle

CUTTING DETAILS

Use the template diagrams on
page 41, adding 6 mm (¼ in)
seam allowance all round each
fabric shape, except where
otherwise indicated. Mark
around the wrong side of the
fabrics.
Template 1 (diamond): 25 in
colour A
Template 1 (diamond): 15 in
colour B
Template 1 (diamond): 10 in
colour C

Template 2 (triangle): 25 in iron-
on interlining (without seam
allowance)
Template 2: 25 in wadding
(without seam allowance)
Template 3 (trunk): 2 in fabric, 1
in interlining (without seam
allowance) and 1 in wadding
(without seam allowance)
Template 4 (pot): 2 in fabric, 1 in
interlining (without seam
allowance) and 1 in wadding
(without seam allowance)

CONSTRUCTION

Place the 25 diamonds cut from
colours B and C wrong side up. Put
one triangle of interlining on the top
half of each, lining up with stitching
and fold lines and ensuring that it is
adhesive side down. Iron on using a
damp cloth to ensure adhesion.

Place a wadding triangle at the other
end of each diamond, lining up with
the stitching and fold lines, pin in
position as shown in diagram 1.
Take one diamond cut in colour A,
place right side up and place one of
the units just made on this, right

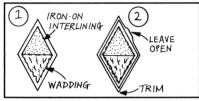

sides together. Stitch by hand or machine around the shape on the stitching lines, just catching in the wadding and leaving an opening along one interlining edge. Trim off the excess fabric at the top and bottom of the diamond (diagram 2). Make 25 units in this manner. Turn all through to the right side. Slip stitch the openings together. *Do not iron* as this will flatten the wadding. Gently pull the diamond into shape and finger press.

Fold the 25 completed diamonds in half, so that colour A is always on the inside and pin together. Arrange the 25 triangles thus made into a tree shape with five triangles in colour B on the base line and four triangles inverted in colour C making up the first row. Continue as shown in diagram 3. Ensure that the triangle with the wadding is on the front of the tree.

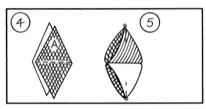

Stitch together in pairs along the fold lines. To do this open out each triangle with colour A on the outside. Stitch, then fold back again as shown in diagrams 4 and 5. Always replace the stitched pairs in their correct position.

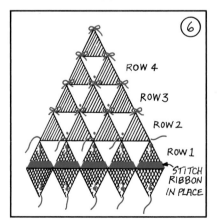

Carefully oversew the triangles together on the back of the tree. Turn the tree to the right side, all the triangles on the front will be hanging free. Stitch a strip of 25 mm (1 in) wide ribbon on the inner edges of the triangles, just above the base fold lines, across the width of the tree on rows 1, 2, 3 and 4, folding the ribbon ends in and stitching them to align with the sloped edges. Catch the upper edge of the ribbon on the construction lines, thus making pockets.

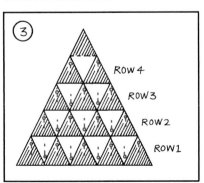

Sew press studs on the points of the six inverted triangles on rows 2, 3 and 4 (diagram 6).

Cut the narrow ribbon into 38 × 15 cm (6 in) lengths and two × 25 cm (10 in) lengths. Knot one end of the short lengths of the ribbon, thread the other end into a tapestry needle, and insert 1 cm (½ in) down from front and back of all the triangle points on row 1, and pull the ribbon through. Repeat on upward-pointing triangles on rows 2, 3 and 4 and on the top triangle. Tie ribbons together into bows.

To make the tree trunk, iron the interlining on to the wrong side of shape 3, lining up with the stitching lines, place wadding over the interlining and place this unit on top of the second shape 3, right sides together. Stitch around the shape, leaving an opening. Turn right side out and slip stitch the opening. Make the 'pot' in the same way, using shape 4. Oversew the trunk to the top of the pot on the wrong side, then oversew the trunk to the tree base on the wrong side.

Place foil-covered chocolate coins in each ribbon pocket and slip bells on to the ribbon bows. Thread one of the two 25 cm (10 in) lengths of ribbon into the tapestry needle and slip through the left base point, thread a bell and tie into a bow. Repeat for the bottom right corner.

Finally make a hanging loop with the remaining narrow ribbon and attach at the back of the tree top.

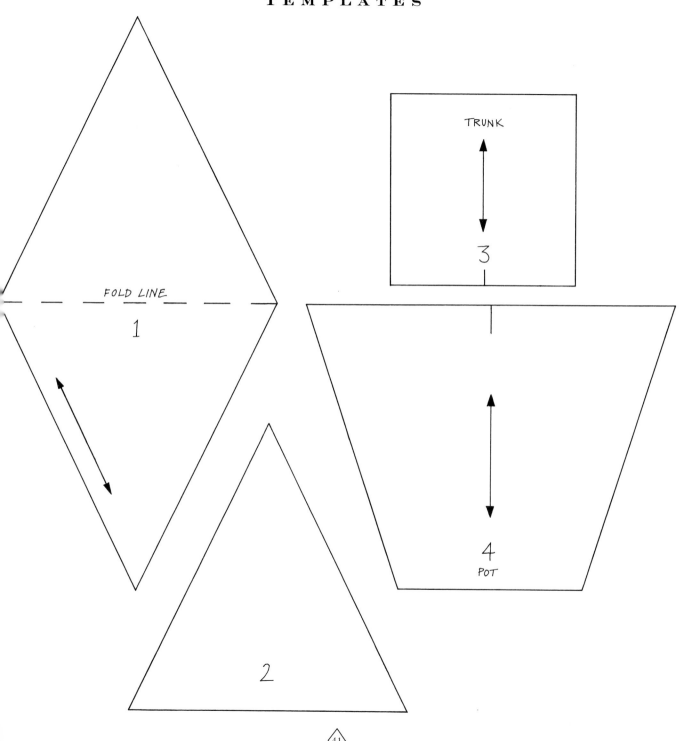

FOLD LINE

1

2

TRUNK

3

4

POT

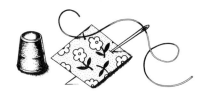

CHRISTMAS STOCKING

Make a stocking for a new baby, or for a child of any age!
It is likely to become a valued part of the Christmas tradition
to be brought out year after year.

REQUIREMENTS

70 cm (¾ yard) cotton fabric for
stocking front and back and
approximately 180 × 5 cm (70
× 2 in) strip cut on bias to bind
stocking (joined as necessary)
70 cm (¾ yard) fabric for lining
70 cm (¾ yard) wadding
5 pieces of fabric approximately
15 × 30 cm (6 × 12 in) for
patchwork, colours A, B, C, D,
E
23 cm (9 in) × 1 cm) (½ in) wide
ribbon for 'tree trunks'
Beads, sequins, lace, etc. for
decoration if desired
Gold thread to embroider name

CUTTING DETAILS

Use templates 1 and 2 on page
45 (enlarged to correct size) to
cut the following, adding 1 cm
(½ in) seam allowance all
round.
Template 1 (stocking back): 1 in
main colour
Template 1: 2 in lining (1
reversed)
Template 1: 2 in wadding
Template 2 (stocking front): 1 in
main colour
Use templates 3 to 6 on page 45
to cut the following, adding
6 mm (¼) turnings all round
each shape (mark centres in
seam allowances) and
extending template 4 to full
size:
Template 3: 8 in colour A
Template 3: 8 in colour B
Template 4: 1 in colour C
Template 5: 4 in colour D
Template 5: 3 in colour E
Template 6: 1 in colour C

CONSTRUCTION

Make up the patchwork for the top
of the stocking, using the seamed
method (page 20) by hand or
machine stitching, thus:

Row 1: alternate four × template 3,
colour A, with three × template 3,
colour B.

Row 2: alternate three × template
3, colour A, with four × template 3,
colour B.

Stitch these two rows together
matching the base points of colour
B in row 1 to the centre of the
triangle, colour B, in second row.
This will create the zig-zag effect.

Row 3: stitch the centre strip
(template 4) to row 2.

Row 4: alternate four × template 5,
colour D, with three × template 5,
colour E. Line up the point of the
centre triangle in this row with the
centre of the patchwork sections in
rows 1 to 3 and stitch (diagram 1,
see next page).

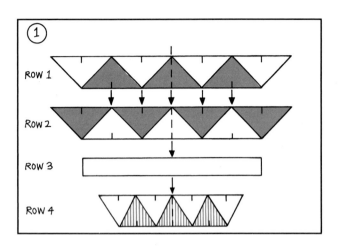

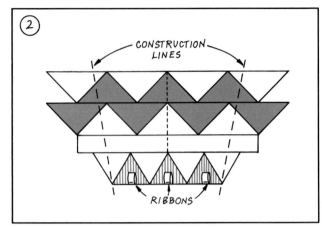

Cut the ribbon into three × 7.5 cm (3 in) lengths, double over and stitch in the middle of the triangles, as shown in diagram 2.

Stitch the patchwork panel to the top of the stocking front (template 2), matching centres, the edges of the patchwork will protrude on the sides, but these will be stitched and trimmed during construction.

Make up the two remaining triangles (template 3) into a square, turn the 6 mm (¼ in) seam

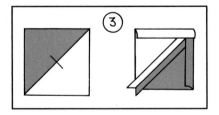

allowance in on two sides (diagram 3) and stitch in position on the stocking front.

Turn in the seam allowance on the straight edge of the toe cap

(template 6), stitch in place. Place the lining, wrong side up on a table, lay the wadding over this, then place the stocking front on top, right side up, and pin together. Tack all layers of the 'sandwich' together, first down the centre, then 1 cm (½ in) in from the edges.

Embroider the chosen name in gold thread, using chain stitch, on the stocking front.

Make a reverse sandwich for the stocking back.

Fold the bias strip in half lengthwise, press gently taking care not to stretch.

With right sides together, tack and stitch the double binding 6 mm (¼ in) in along the top of both stocking sections. Cut the strip to fit. Fold the excess over to the wrong side and slip stitch in place.

Place the front and back stocking sections *wrong sides together*, tack and stitch through all the layers just

inside the stitching line into the seam allowances marked on the back section. Trim the patchwork section and all the seam allowances to 6 mm (¼ in).

Tack and stitch the remaining double binding all round the stocking, making a hanging loop at the back. Fold the binding over and slip stitch on to the back, covering the stitching.

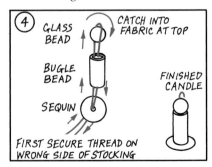

Add lace and decorations as desired. For example, to make 'candles' follow diagram 4.

N.B. Do not put beads and sequins on a young child's stocking.

TEMPLATES

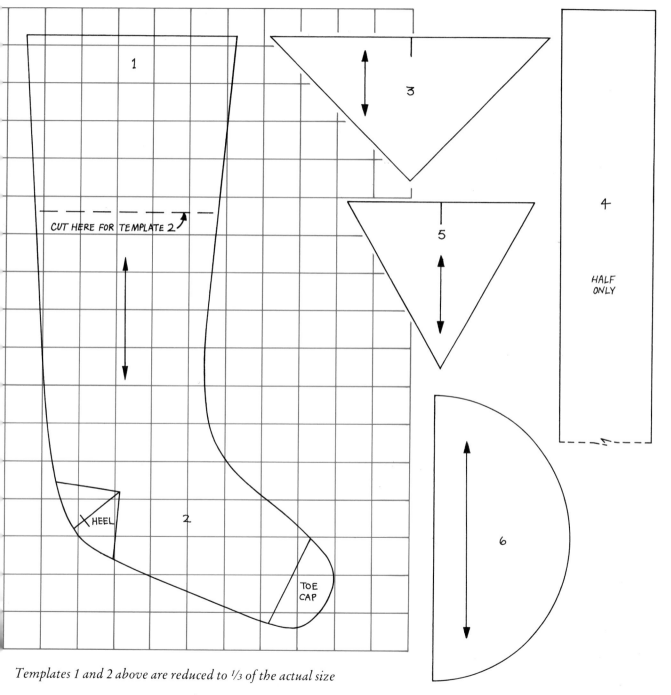

1

CUT HERE FOR TEMPLATE 2

2

HEEL

TOE CAP

3

5

4

HALF ONLY

6

Templates 1 and 2 above are reduced to ⅓ of the actual size

POLESCREEN

A decorative marriage of needlework skill and design
with the tradition of furniture craftsmanship. An opportunity,
perhaps, to use those precious tiny pieces of rare fabrics,
which have been saved for something special.

This design, featuring a diamond-shaped panel with four fans in a striped surround, is suitable for a polescreen or a firescreen or it could be framed as a picture.

In the polescreen shown in the photograph colour B was not used in the border shapes, but a sixth colour in a darker shade was added to enhance the colour scheme of the fans.

REQUIREMENTS

25 cm (¼ yard) each of silk in 6
   colours*
50 cm (½ yard) white felt
50 cm (½ yard) × 2 oz wadding
Tube of liquid latex glue
Packet of 8 mm (⅜ in) fine tacks
Upholstery braid (see method)

* If the work is to be mounted
into a polescreen frame, an extra
70 cm (¾ yard) of one of the silks
will be required for the backing.

CUTTING DETAILS

Use the template diagrams on
   page 49, adding 6 mm (¼ in)
   seam allowance all round each
   fabric shape. Draw round the
   templates on the wrong side of
   the fabrics.
Template 1: 4 in colour A
Template 1: 8 in colour B
Template 1: 8 in colour C
Template 2: 4 in colour D
Template 3: 4 in colour E
Template 3 (reversed): 4 in
   colour E

CONSTRUCTION

Pin all the patchwork shapes out on a board in the correct sequence (diagram 1). Using the seamed method (page 20), stitch along the marked lines only, pin and stitch 1C to 1B, then add 1A, 1B and 1C to complete the fan arc. Press the seam allowances both the same way, away from the centre of the fan (diagram 2).

Tack the curved edge of shape 2D to the wrong side along the marked line and slip stitch in place at the base of the arc on the right side (diagram 3).

Seam one shape 3E and one 3E (reversed) together, matching notches.

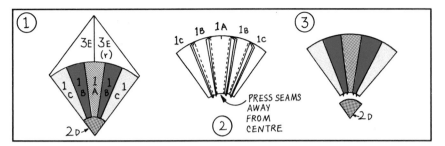

Pin this section to the completed fan, taking care to match the base of seam E to the centre of the fan. Pin at the corners, then ease the concave and convex curves together between the pins and stitch. Press the seam down on to the fan (diagram 4).

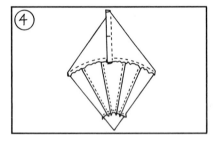

Make all four diamond shapes in this manner. Seam together in pairs, then the pairs together to make a large diamond (diagram 5).

It will now be necessary to enlarge this panel to fit your particular

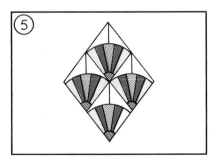

screen. Using the backing panel of your frame or screen, make a paper pattern of the complete backing. Remember to leave an extra allowance on the outer edges to enable the fabric to be secured to the back of the frame. Mark the centre vertical and horizontal lines, then the outline diamond shape of the patchwork panel, positioned in the centre, matching the four points of the diamond to the centre lines. These corner pieces are the templates 4, 5, 6 and 7 (diagram 6).

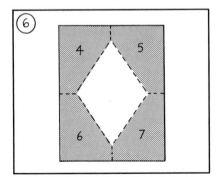

Cut strips of silk in varying widths (cutting four strips of identical width from each colour).

N.B. Colour B in the fans was not used in the corner sections but a sixth, darker colour was added.

Machine stitch these strips together in the same sequence for each corner piece (they will run parallel to the diagonal edge of each corner), until the textiles thus made are large enough to cover the templates. Ensure that the four corner pieces fit their respective templates, as the side edges are longer than the top

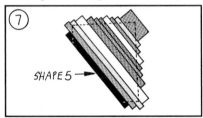

and bottom edges (diagram 7). Press all the seams the same way.

Stitch these corners to the central diamond to create a rectangle with diamond-shaped 'frames' around the central panel (diagram 8).

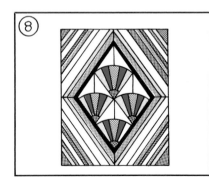

To mount the work, cut white felt to the same size as the back panel of the frame without any seam allowance. Smear with latex glue, leave until almost dry, then stick to the back panel. (If too much adhesive is used it will seep through

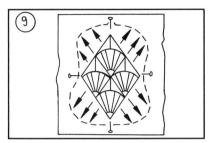

the felt and could spoil the finished product.) Cut the wadding to the same size and place on the felt.

Lay the completed patchwork panel on top of the wadding, being careful to match centres to centre top, base and sides of frame. Gently smooth from the centre of the patchwork panel, taking care not to distort the

design, then, using fine tacks, tap the tacks part way in, making sure they are clear of the visible area of the polescreen and checking that the design is central and without puckers (diagram 9).

If the work is to be mounted in a picture frame, the excess fabric can be taken to the back and secured with masking tape, then covered by paper after insertion in the frame. Remove the temporary tacks before fitting in the frame.

If, however, the piece is to be viewed from both sides, carefully tack the excess fabric to the reverse of the back panel, then trim off the

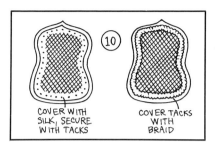

excess. Remove the temporary tacks, then cover the back with silk and tack in place around the edge. Trim, then cover the tack heads with upholstery braid (diagram 10). Carefully glue the upholstery braid in place, following the adhesive manufacturer's instructions. Insert the panel into the frame.

TEMPLATES

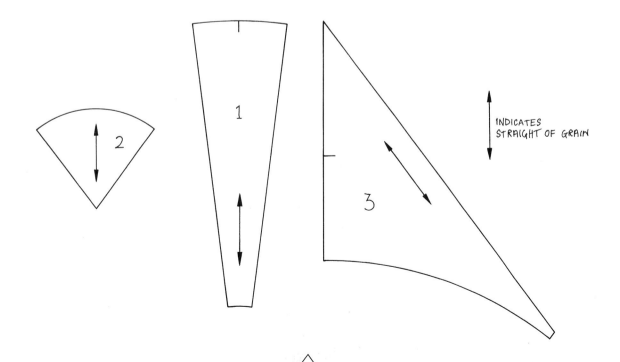

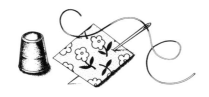

BUILD A QUILT

Patchwork quilts are often made in traditional North American 'block' designs, that is units of design which can be used on their own or, more usually, repeated to create an overall design.

Many blocks fit into grids, i.e. 4 patch, 5 patch, 7 patch, 8 pointed stars (see design sheet, page 53). Note that having drawn the design on to the basic grid, some of the original divisions can be removed, allowing a better-shaped template to be made. These drafting-only lines are shown as dotted lines on the diagram.

Take a little time to plan the overall design of the patchwork. Choose the block you wish to use and think how it is to be repeated, will it be set square, on point, alternated with another design or a plain square, should it be sashed? Refer to the planning sheet featuring the Variable Star block for just some of the variations. Graph paper can be used for many designs both for the scale plan of the patchwork as well as for the actual size drafting of the block and its templates, but isometric paper would be required for hexagons, 60° diamonds,

equilateral triangles, etc., and plain paper for designs based on 8 pointed stars (see page 17).

Having planned the patchwork, draft one of the blocks to the exact size required, using the grid system, cutting the templates and fabrics as detailed in Skill File, page 19.

The Sampler Quilt photographed has fifteen traditional patchwork blocks set on point, alternating with plain squares and triangles; it has been finished with two borders and quilted. At first sight all fifteen blocks look very different, although there are two versions of the Mariner's Compass. Look carefully, however, at the blocks in the top left hand and top right hand corners: these are both Castle Wall and made from exactly the same template shapes, but because of the way the fabrics have been used a totally different effect is achieved. Note particularly the use of the striped fabric.

The blocks featured are, starting from the top row and working down always from left to right:

Castle Wall 1 *
Star within a Star
Castle Wall 2
Union
Mariner's Compass 1
Corn and Beans
1904 Star
Mariner's Compass 2
Judy in Arabia
Swing in the Centre
Double Wedding Ring
St Louis Star *
Queen Charlotte's Crown *
Variable Star *
Log Cabin variation

* Template patterns and stitching sequences are given for these blocks on the following pages. All the blocks measure 30 × 30 cm (12 × 12 in). Double Wedding Ring and Log Cabin design variations are used in following projects.

To join the patches, use the seamed method (page 20), stitching by hand or machine.

Assembling blocks into patchwork top

Use this basic system to stitch any top together, remembering that it is always easier to stitch in straight lines. Blocks with diagonal designs will be sewn in diagonal strips.

When sashing (or setting), cut the horizontal strips to the finished length of the block, plus 6 mm (¼ in) seam allowances all round.

N.B. Establish the length of the block by measuring through the centres both vertically and horizontally. The actual edge of the block does not give an accurate measurement because of all the seam allowances and raw edges of the fabric which can stretch.

Cut the vertical sashing strips to the length of the number of blocks in the vertical row *plus* the finished widths of the horizontal sashing

strips, *plus* 6 mm (¼ in) seam allowances all round. Mark where the seams of the horizontal sashing strips will meet the vertical strips in the seam allowance on both edges. This will ensure that all the blocks are in alignment. Stitch in position. Add this unit to rows 2 and 3. In diagram 1, rows 2 and 3 have already been joined either side of a vertical strip.

Borders

Measure the patchwork top through the centres as described above.

Cut the border strips to this length *plus* twice the width of the borders *plus* 6 mm (¼ in) seam allowance all round.

Mark the border strips and the patchwork top with pins aligning as shown in diagram 2. Lay the border strips onto the patchwork top, right sides together, matching pins, tack, and stitch in position on all four sides. Press seam allowances onto

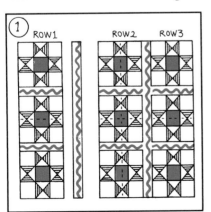

border, leaving two overlapping tails on each corner (diagram 3).

Lay the corner of the patchwork carefully on the table, with the tails lying at right angles to each other.

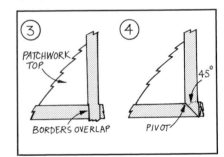

Take the top one and fold it underneath at an angle of 45°, pivoting on the stitching point. Tack the mitre thus formed, stitch, then trim away the excess fabric (diagram 4).

If the patchwork is to be quilted, see Skill File, page 88.

For finishing suggestions, see Skill File, page 89.

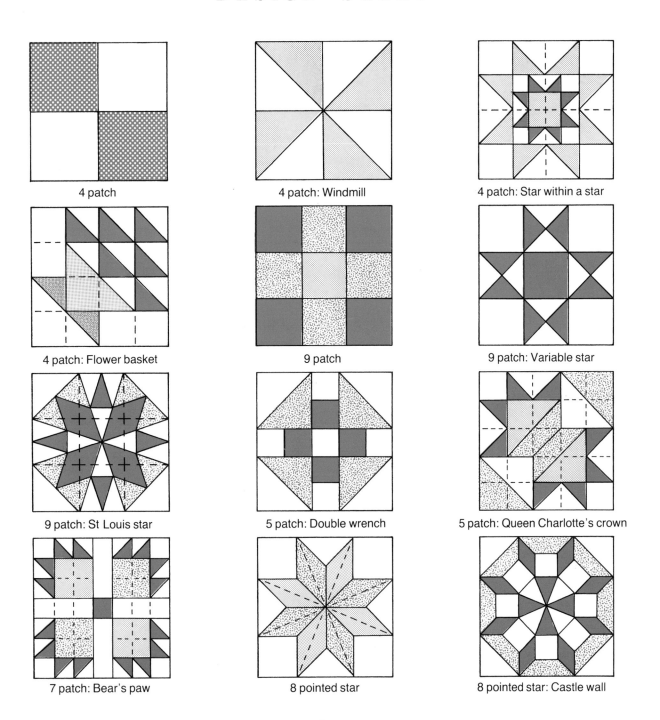

4 patch

4 patch: Windmill

4 patch: Star within a star

4 patch: Flower basket

9 patch

9 patch: Variable star

9 patch: St Louis star

5 patch: Double wrench

5 patch: Queen Charlotte's crown

7 patch: Bear's paw

8 pointed star

8 pointed star: Castle wall

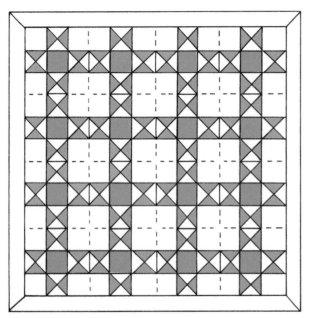

Blocks set together

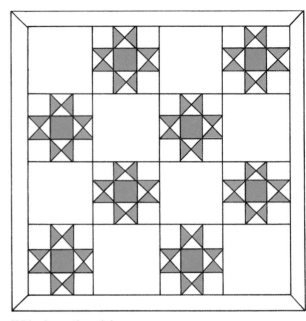

With alternating plain squares

Blocks on point

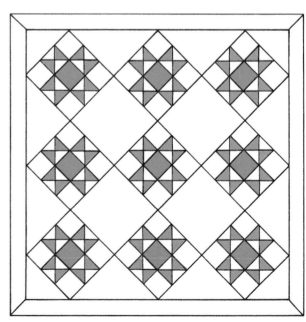

With alternating plain squares

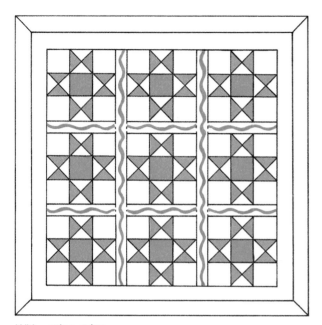

With setting strips

With the colours in different sequences

With setting strips

A medallion centre with 2 blocks

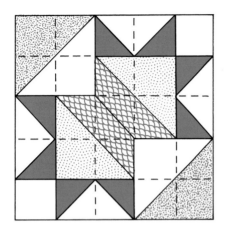

QUEEN CHARLOTTE'S CROWN

A 5 patch (5 × 5) block, finished size 30 cm (12 in) square

CUTTING DETAILS

Use templates 1 to 5, adding 6 mm (¼ in) seam allowance all round each fabric shape.
Template 1: 4 in colour A
Template 2: 8 in colour B
Template 3: 2 in colour A
Template 4: 2 in colour A
Template 4: 2 in colour C
Template 4: 2 in colour D
Template 5: 2 in colour C

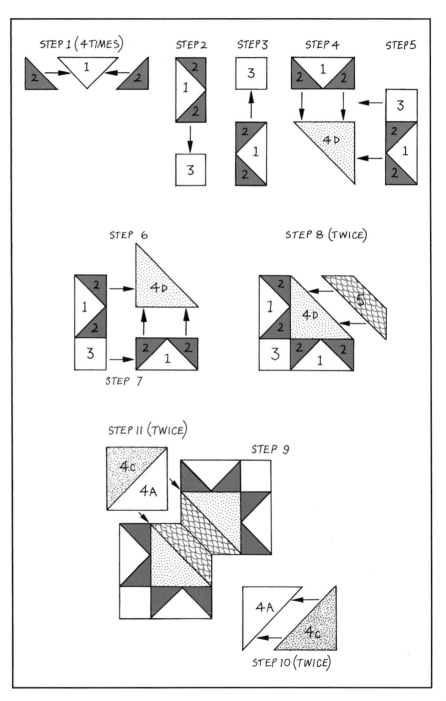

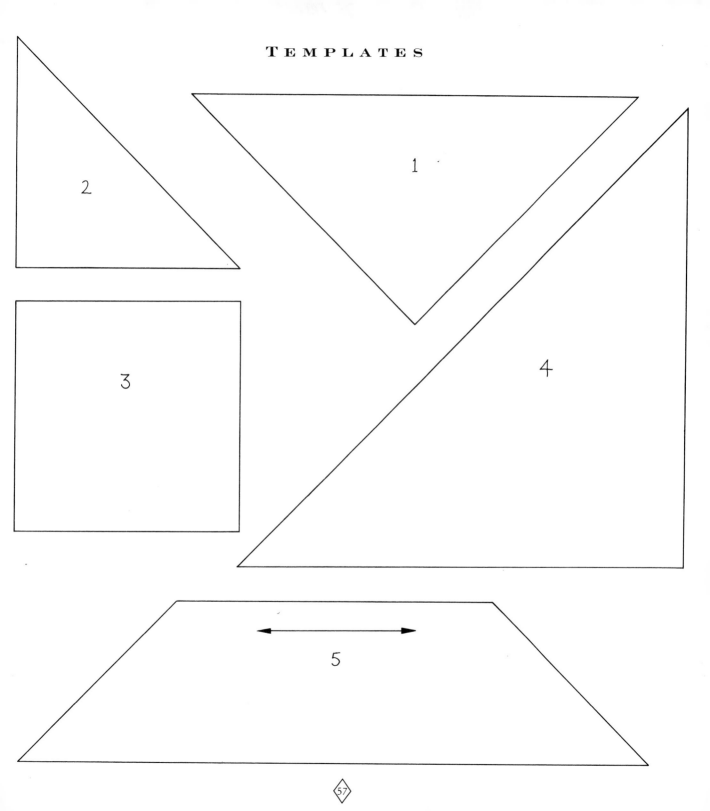

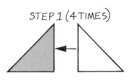

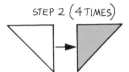

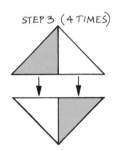

VARIABLE STAR

A 9 patch block set on point,
finished size 30 cm (12 in) square

CUTTING DETAILS

Use templates 1 and 2, adding
6 mm (¼ in) seam allowance
all round each fabric shape.
Template 1: 8 in colour A
Template 1: 8 in colour B
Template 2: 4 in colour A
Template 2: 1 in colour B

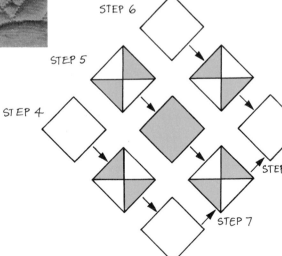

TEMPLATES

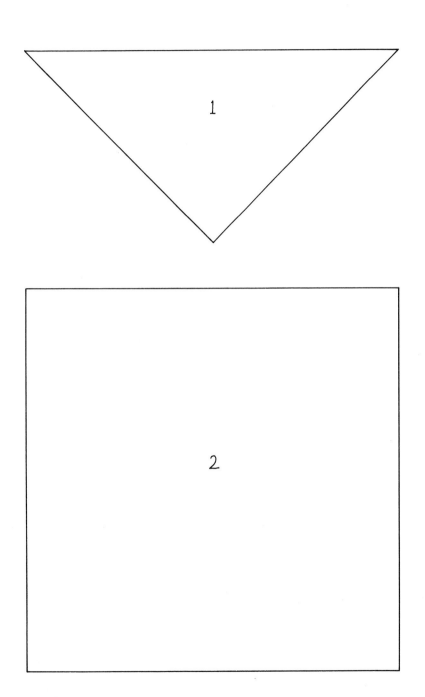

1

2

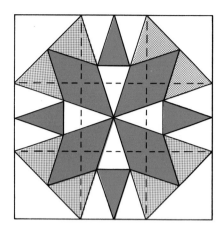

St Louis star

A 9 patch block, finished size 30 cm (12 in) square

Cutting details

Use templates 1 to 4, adding 6 mm (¼ in) seam allowance all round each fabric shape.
Template 1: 12 in colour A
Template 1: 4 in colour B
Template 2: 8 in colour C
Template 3: 4 in colour A
Template 4: 4 in colour B

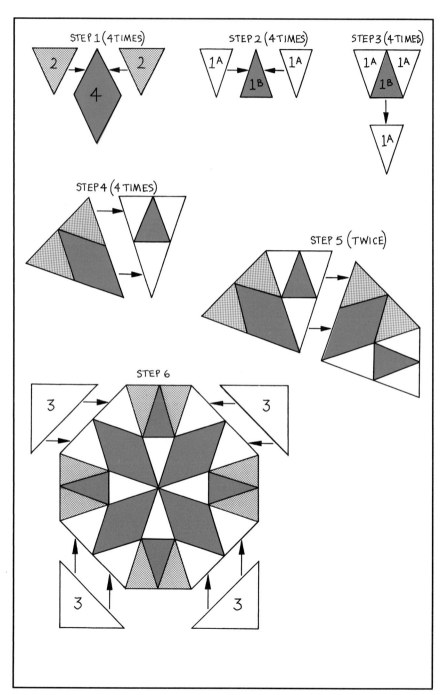

TEMPLATES

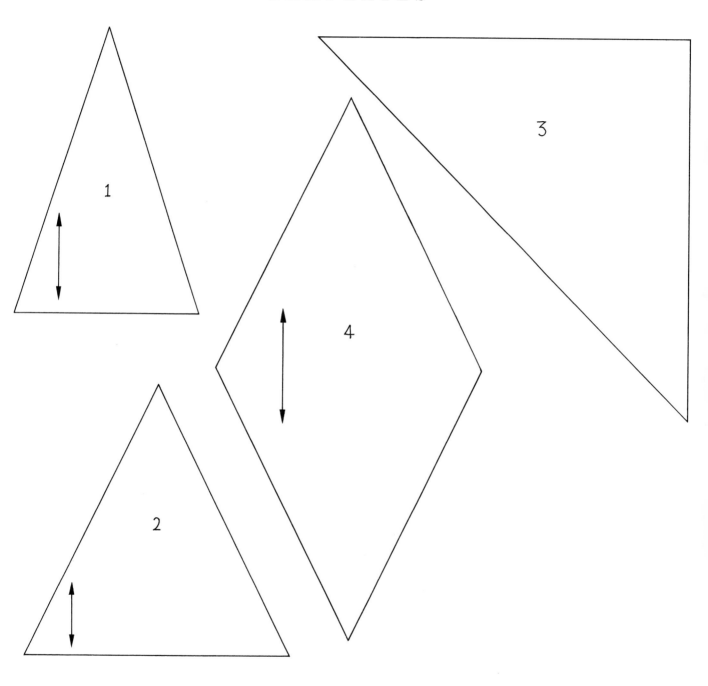

CASTLE WALL

Based on the 8 pointed star, finished size 30 cm (12 in) square. Two versions on point are shown.

CUTTING DETAILS

Use templates 1 to 5, adding
  6 mm (¼ in) seam allowance
  all round each fabric shape.
Template 1: 8 in colour C
Template 2: 8 in colour A
Template 3: 4 in colour A
Template 3: 4 in colour B
Template 4: 8 in colour B
Template 5: 4 in colour A

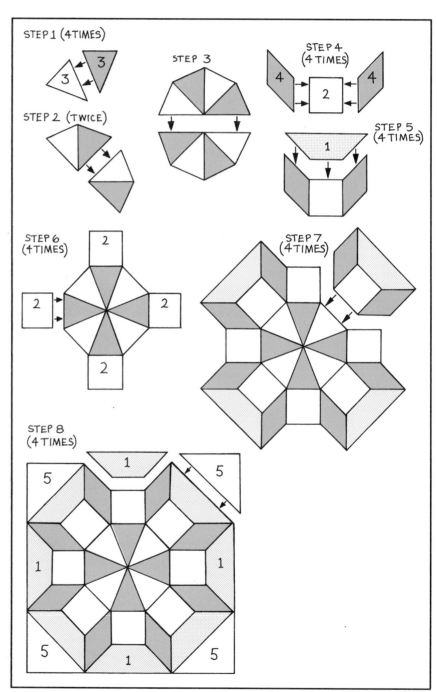

TEMPLATES

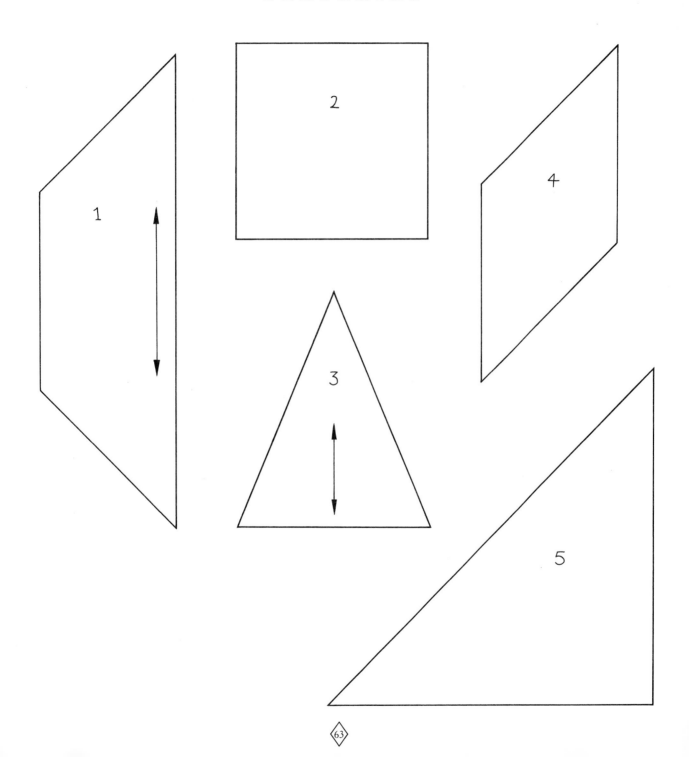

LOG CABIN

Log Cabin, perhaps the most famous of the traditional
American patchworks, conjures up the emotional feel of the trek
to the West, of the need to make a home and a living.
This is a thrifty form of patchwork ideally suited to the
hoarded, best-loved fabric remnants.

The most common form of Log Cabin is a series of light and dark strips of fabric spiralling around a central square, traditionally red (denoting the fireplace) or yellow (the lighted window). This gives a diagonal light and dark effect to the basic block. Any number of strips can be used, but the instructions below use three light, three dark and a larger centre square. The finished block measures 15 × 15 cm (6 × 6 in).

The coverlet photographed on page 66 was made from fine woollen fabrics stitched onto a foundation square. It has 48 squares each 18 × 18 cm (7 × 7 in), using three light and three dark fabrics around a red centre square, all 2.5 cm (1 in) finished width, arranged in the Barn Raising pattern. Black borders 5 cm (2 in) wide have been added and the coverlet backed. The patchwork is attached to the backing on the corner of each block.

REQUIREMENTS

For each 15 cm (6 in) block the fabric needed is as follows:
Centre square: a piece 5.2 × 5.2 cm (2 × 2 in)
1st & 2nd dark strips made from same fabric: a strip 3.2 × 12.2 cm (1¼ × 4¾ in)
1st & 2nd light strips made from

same fabric: a strip 3.2 × 16 cm (1¼ × 6¼ in)
3rd & 4th dark strips made from same fabric: a strip 3.2 × 20 cm (1¼ × 7¾ in)
3rd & 4th light strips made from same fabric: a strip 3.2 × 23.5 cm (1¼ × 9¼ in)

5th & 6th dark strips made from same fabric: a strip 3.2 × 27.5 cm (1¼ × 10¾ in)
5th & 6th light strips made from same fabric: a strip 3.2 × 31.5 cm (1¼ × 12¼ in)

Design 1 – Light and Dark

It is the manner in which these blocks are assembled which gives the patchwork its interest.

Preparation for hand sewing:
Cut a strip template 2 cm (¾ in) wide and about 38 cm (15 in) long. Mark three light and three dark fabrics, on the wrong side, adding 6 mm (¼ in) seam allowances along both long edges of each strip. Cut all the strips of fabric as long as possible by moving the template along the fabric. Wherever possible, cut these strips on the straight of grain, i.e. parallel to the selvage, to help prevent the fabric from stretching. If not possible, cut the strips at right angles to the selvage.

Cut a centre square template 4 × 4 cm (1½ × 1½ in). Mark the chosen fabric, adding 6 mm (¼ in) seam allowance all round.

Pin, matching seam lines, and stitch along the marked line, following either method (a) or (b) below.

Preparation for machine sewing:
Cut a strip template 38 cm (15 in) long and 3.2 cm (1¼ in) wide (that is 2 cm + 2 × 6 mm for seams/¾ in + 2 × ¼ in). Also add 6 mm (¼ in) to the centre square as above and cut. The machine foot will be used as a seam allowance guide as detailed in the Seminole Patchwork section (page 76). Mark and cut three light and three dark fabrics as described under hand sewing.

Stitching sequence for both hand and machine methods:

Method (a) without foundation square

When using firmly-woven cotton fabrics, the seamed method of construction is satisfactory.

N.B. It is important to press after the addition of every strip to ensure the block remains square.

Place the first light fabric right sides together along one side of the centre square. Stitch right across the full length, trim the strip to the same

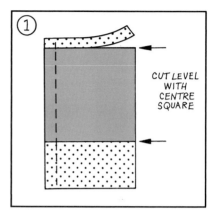

length as the square (diagram 1). Open out, then press the seams both the same way, away from the centre square (diagram 2).

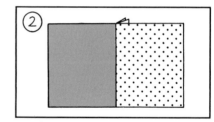

CUTTING LINE

STITCHING LINE

LOG CABIN STRIP TEMPLATE

32 mm (1¼")   ¾" 20 mm

Using the same light fabric, right sides together, stitch across the end

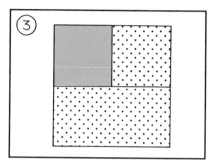

of the light strip and the second side of the centre square (diagram 3). Trim, open and press as before. Using the first dark fabric, stitch across the end of the second light

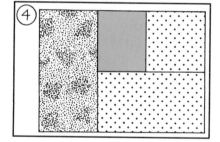

strip and the third side of the centre square, trim, open out, press (diagram 4).

Using the same dark fabric, stitch across the end of the first dark fabric strip, the centre square and the first light strip (diagram 5).

The centre square will now be enclosed by two light strips and two dark strips. Continue round the square using the second light fabric twice, second dark twice, third light twice and third dark twice,

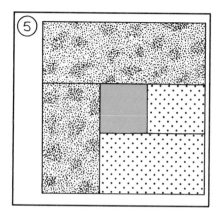

trimming each strip before opening and pressing. Also remember to go around the centre square in the same direction, all clockwise or all anticlockwise.

The completed block will be 16.2 cm (6½ in) square, i.e. with 6 mm (¼ in) seam allowance all round (diagram 6).

Make the required number of blocks for your chosen design in the same manner.

To assemble the blocks, lay them out on the floor or table in the chosen sequence or pin them to a large sheet. If you are unable to complete sewing all the blocks together at one time, they can be rolled up in the sheet. Refer to the planning sheet featuring the Light and Dark block for some of the variations possible.

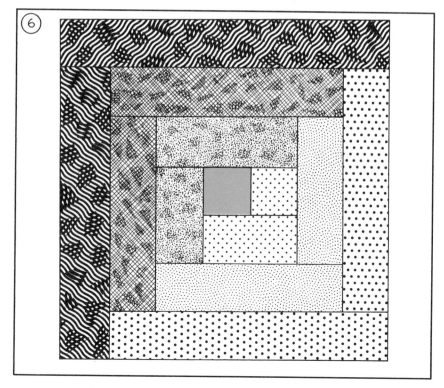

Join the blocks into strips, then join the strips together, being careful to match the corners of the blocks.

Method (b) – with foundation square

If silk, fine wool or mixed fabrics (e.g. Viyella) are to be used, mount the fabrics on to a foundation square. This will give strength and stability to the block.

Cut a foundation square 18 × 18 cm (7 × 7 in) in a fine white or natural-coloured cotton fabric, so that it will not show through the Log Cabin fabrics. Draw diagonal lines from corner to corner.

Tack the centre square in position, matching its corners to the diagonal lines.

Cut the first light strip so that it is long enough to go along the edge of the centre square. Lay along this edge, right sides together, then stitch in position through all layers. Press open (diagram 7).

Measuring and trimming the length of each strip, build up around the central square as detailed in method (a), but stitching through all layers and pressing open at each addition, until the three light and three dark strips have been added alternately. When the block is complete, tack

around the outer edges and trim away the excess foundation fabric.

Make the required number of blocks, assemble as detailed previously, stitching through the foundation fabric as well as the patchwork strips.

Design 2 – Courthouse Steps

This Log Cabin variation still uses three light and three dark fabrics but they are built up in pairs on opposite sides of the central square, as shown in diagram 8.

Depending on the fabrics chosen, it can be made using method (a) or (b). It is still very important that

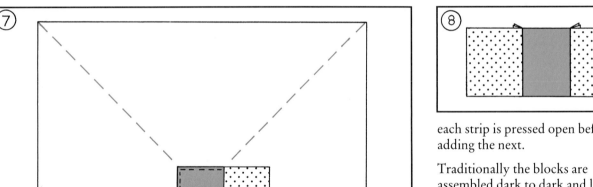

each strip is pressed open before adding the next.

Traditionally the blocks are assembled dark to dark and light to light, giving an impression of hour glasses or Chinese lanterns, so this design does not afford as many variations in assembly as the diagonal light and dark design. Refer to the planning sheet for a grouping of nine blocks.

Border details are given on page 52, quilting instructions (if desired) on page 88 and finishing ideas on page 89.

Courthouse steps

Straight furrow

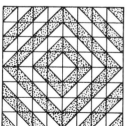

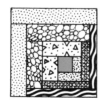

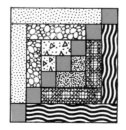

Barn raising – top: 16
blocks; above: 64 blocks

Thick & thin strips
variation

Corner stones variation

Light & dark

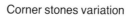

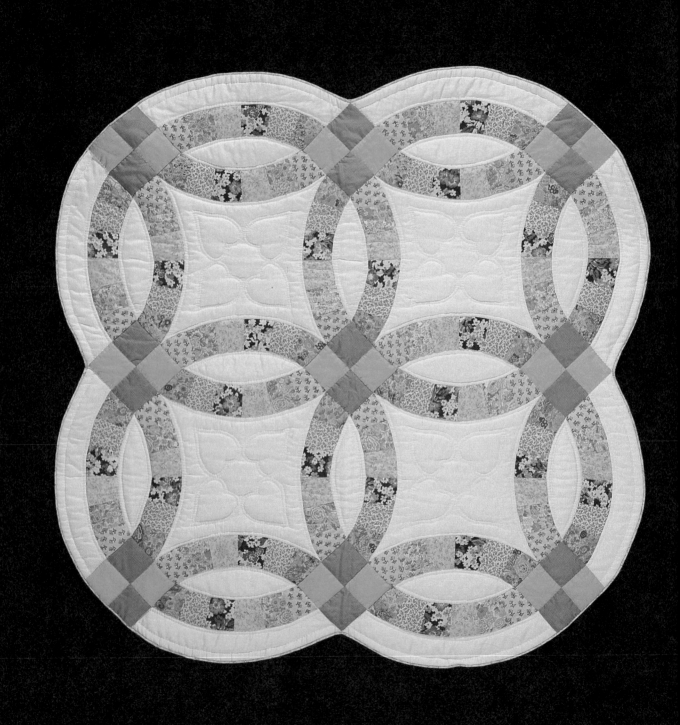

DOUBLE WEDDING RING THROW

A 1930s curved seam patchwork design, said to test a
needleworker's skill, but which, with careful cutting and
stitching, is really no more difficult than any other.

The templates and cutting scheme given below
will make a 45 cm (18 in) diameter circle. With
the addition of a frill or gusset this could be
made into a round cushion. Alternatively, use
a half or quarter of the large template, to form
a square cushion, as shown in diagram 8.

If making a larger piece, such as the 'throw'
illustrated, a number of complete circles are
constructed and linked with centre panels and
additional arcs. To assess the amount of fabric
needed for the main colour (templates 1 and 2),
measure the finished size of the complete
project. This will allow for the seam
allowances around each template (diagram 6).

REQUIREMENTS

Fabric amounts are for the 45 cm
(18 in) diameter circle.
50 cm (½ yard) in colour A
4 different patterned fabrics (B,
C, D, E): each piece 30 ×
15 cm (12 × 6 in) for
template 3
2 different patterned fabrics (F,
G): each piece 30 × 15 cm (12
× 6 in) for template 4
2 different plain fabrics (H, I):
each piece 30 × 7.5 cm (12 ×
3 in) for template 5

CUTTING DETAILS

Use the template diagrams on
page 75, adding 6 mm (¼ in)
seam allowances all round
each shape. See below for
how to construct template 1.
Template 1: 1 in colour A
Template 2: 4 in colour A
(Mark centres in seam
allowance, as shown on
templates)
Template 3: 8 in colour B
Template 3: 8 in colour C
Template 3: 8 in colour D
Template 3: 8 in colour E
Template 4: 8 in colour F
Template 4 (reversed): 8 in
colour G
(On shapes cut from templates 3
and 4 mark notches as
indicated.)
Template 5: 4 in colour H
Template 5: 4 in colour I

To make template 1, fold a 38 cm (15 in) square of tracing paper into quarters. Line up the fold lines with the dotted lines on the quarter template and mark the curved lines. Cut while still folded, this will give a complete template when opened

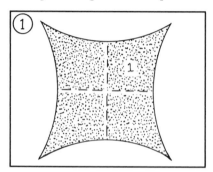

out (diagram 1). Attach the tracing paper template to a piece of thin card with a little glue stick and cut out the card.

This design can be sewn by the seamed method (page 20), either by hand or machine.

Lay one each of the four fabrics cut from template 3 in the chosen sequence on a cork tile (page 15). Pin together (diagram 2a).

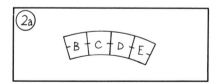

Add the shapes cut from template 4 and template 4 reversed to each end of the arc, matching notches on straight edges. Pin and stitch together along the marked lines (diagram 2b).

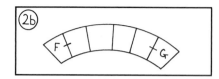

Construct the eight arcs using the same sequence.

Press the seam allowances all the same way, being very careful not to stretch the fabrics.

Pin the inner edges of the arcs either side of shape 2, matching centre seam of arc to the notches on shape 2. Stitch along the marked lines, taking great care at the points on

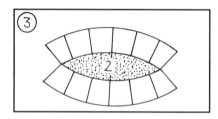

shape 2 (diagram 3). Press the seam allowances on to the arc. Make four units in this manner.

Pin the outer edge of the arcs to shape 1, matching centre mark on shape 1 to centre seam of the arc. Stitch carefully along the marked lines only (diagram 4). Press the seam allowances on to the arc. Attach three more arcs to the remaining three sides in the same manner.

N.B. Care must be taken when attaching shapes 1 and 2, because concave curves have to be sewn to convex curves. This should be

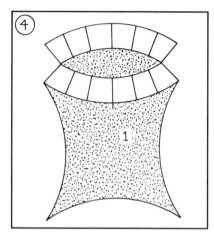

achieved without clipping the curves, which can leave weak areas.

If only the one 45 cm (18 in) circle is being made, the squares (template 5) are added at this stage. To do this, stitch squares H and I into four pairs. Tie the junctions of the arcs together on the right side as shown in diagram 5. These are temporary and will be removed when the piecing is completed. With right sides together, match the stitching line at point (a) to point (a) at the junction of the arcs, also matching the seam line on the squares to point (b), as shown in diagram 5. Stitch in

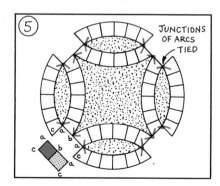

position, then match points (c) on the arc to points (c) on the squares, stitch together.

N.B. Treat each of these as single seams, do not try to stitch round the corners.

Snip away the ties.

If, however, a larger item is to be made, make up the units as shown

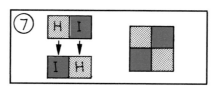

in diagram 6. The squares are inserted when the otherwise finished patchwork has been sewn together, as follows:

Stitch squares H and I together in

pairs, then stitch the pairs together into squares (diagram 7). Next match points (a), (b) and (c), as before, but this time joining two rings together. Stitch in position.

Alternative method: Make the square as above. Cut some thin white card to the finished size of this 4-square patch. Lay the card on the wrong side of the fabric patch, matching edges to the stitching line. Damp the edges with a little spray starch. (Spray some starch into a saucer and use fingers.) Fold the seam allowances over the card and iron until dry. Remove the card. This will give a firm, accurate square which can be applied on the right side of the patchwork and slip stitched in place.

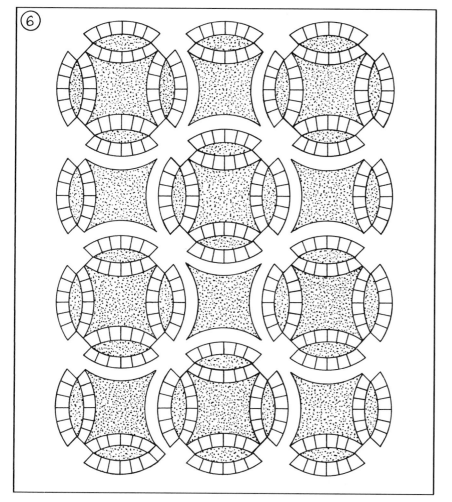

A Double Wedding Ring patchwork being quilted

TEMPLATES

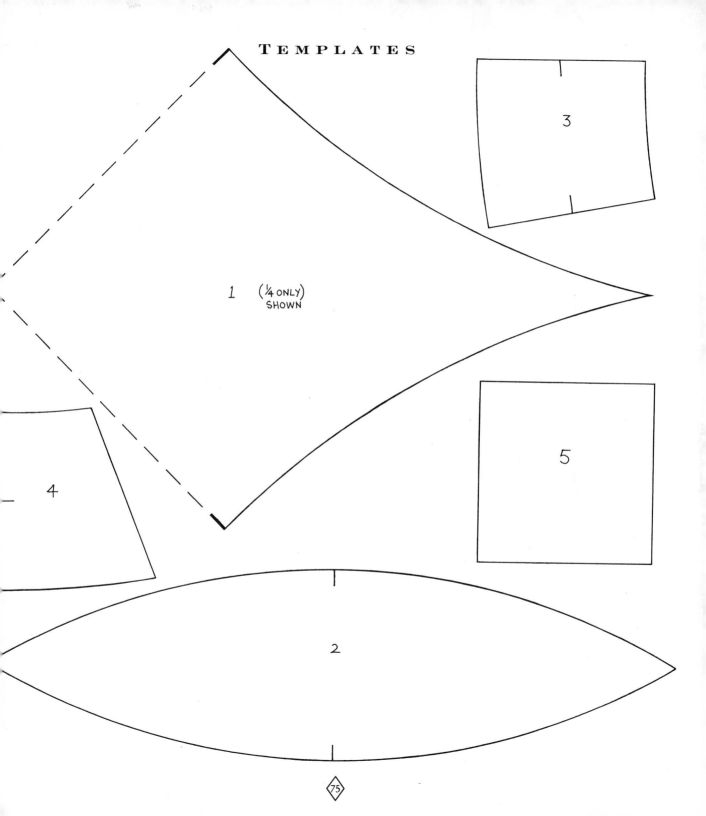

1 (¼ ONLY) SHOWN

2

3

4

5

Seminole and Strip Patchwork

The Seminole Indians of Florida have given
their name to a distinctive form of patchwork. It is a series of
fabric strips, *machine* stitched together, then cut into
sections, and resewn to form seemingly complicated designs.
This patchwork is extremely adaptable and can be
used for clothes, soft furnishings and quilts. The instructions
given are for three arrangements but the variations,
with a little imagination, are limitless.

Strip Patchwork can be seen as a variation of the Seminole method, as it utilizes the concept of machine stitching strips of fabric together and recutting the resultant textile, but this time using a larger template, as in the cot quilt and cushion photographed on page 78.

CONSTRUCTION

Take care when putting the fabrics together that the cut edges align exactly, use the outer edge of the machine presser foot as a guide, lining it up to the fabric edges, then stitch together. This should automatically give a 6 mm (¼ in) seam (diagram 1a). If your presser foot is very narrow, measure 6 mm (¼ in) to the right of the needle position and stick a piece of

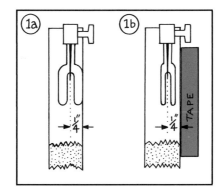

coloured tape on the machine base (diagram 1b).

When sewing strips together, stitch seams in alternating directions. This will help to prevent the fabric from curving. Press each seam allowance open as you go.

This method of working has been used for the Roman Stripe cot quilt and the Rail Fence strip cushion.

SEMINOLE PATCHWORK STITCHING
AND CUTTING SEQUENCE 1

Cut the strips 37 mm (1½ in) wide –
i.e. 25 mm (1 in) finished width.
Set 1: cut 3 in colour A and 2 in
colour B
Set 2: cut 2 in colour A and 3 in
colour B

Machine the sets together as shown
in diagrams 1 and 2, then cut again
into strips 37 mm (1½ in) wide at
right angles to previous strips.
Assemble by stitching alternate
strips from sets 1 and 2 together
(diagram 3).

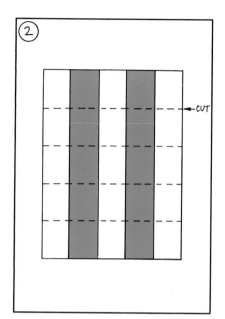

CUTTING DETAILS

Whenever possible, cut the
strips on the straight of
grain, i.e. parallel to the
selvage. This helps to
prevent stretching and
distortion. Mark and cut the
strips accurately with the
seam allowance added. It is
not necessary to mark the
stitching line.

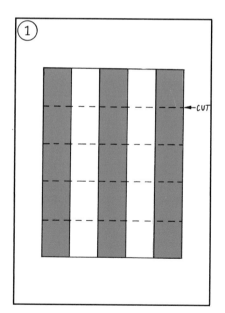

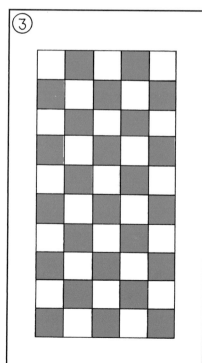

SEMINOLE PATCHWORK STITCHING
AND CUTTING SEQUENCE 2

Cut nine strips of fabric each 37 mm
(1½ in) wide – 25 mm (1 in) finished
width. When stitched together, cut
strips at right angles, 37 mm (1½ in)
wide, as shown in diagram 4.

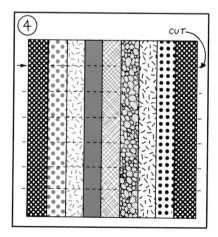

Stitch the strips together, dropping down one strip as shown in diagram 5. This will give the diagonal effect. Cut off the triangular section at the bottom and stitch to the top, matching as before to make a rectangle.

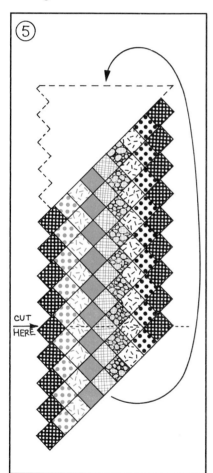

SEMINOLE PATCHWORK STITCHING AND CUTTING SEQUENCE 3

Set 1: cut 2 strips in colour A, 52 mm (2 in) wide – 40 mm (1½ in) finished width

Cut 1 strip in colour B, 22 mm (1 in) wide – 10 mm (½ in) finished width

Set 2: cut 2 strips in colour C, 52 mm (2 in) wide – 40 mm (1½ in) finished width

Cut 1 strip in colour D, 22 mm (1 in) wide – 10 mm (½ in) finished width

When the two sets are machined together, cut into further strips at an angle of 45° as shown (diagram 6), reversing the angle on the second strip (diagram 7). Assemble the alternate strips vertically as shown in diagram 8 and trim off the points to make a rectangle.

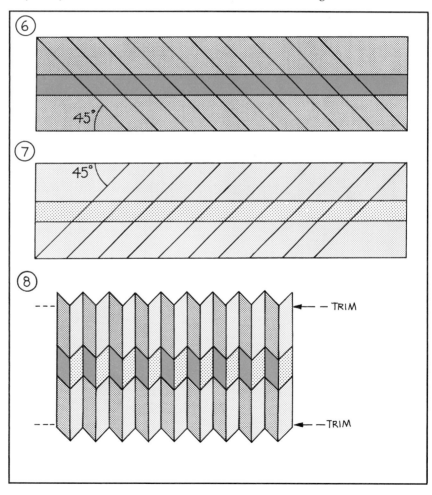

STRIP PATCHWORK 1 – ROMAN
STRIPES

Cut four strips 37 mm (1½ in) wide
– 25 mm (1 in) finished width.
Machine together. Using the
triangle template, mark and cut as
shown in diagram 1, adding 6 mm
(¼ in) seam allowances.

Stitch one triangle made from strips
to one triangle cut from plain fabric

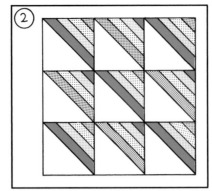

together along the longest sides to
form a square. Group the squares as
shown in diagram 2. Stitch together.

Cot Quilt
The Roman Stripe Cot Quilt in the
photograph is made from 35 blocks
each made from one plain and one
striped triangle assembled in rows
of 5 × 7 blocks, surrounded by two
borders – finished width 5 cm (2 in)
and 2 cm (¾ in) – and mitred at the
corners. The quilting is simply 'in
the ditch' (page 89) and the quilt is
completed with a piped edge (page
90). The overall dimensions are
approximately 82 cm (32 in) wide by
110 cm (43 in) long.

STRIP PATCHWORK 2 – RAIL FENCE

Cut four strips 37 mm (1½ in) wide
– 25 mm (1 in) finished width.
Machine together. Using the square
template, mark and cut as shown in
diagram 3, adding 6 mm (¼ in) seam
allowances.

Assemble as shown in diagram 4.

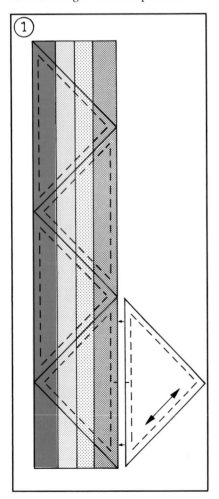

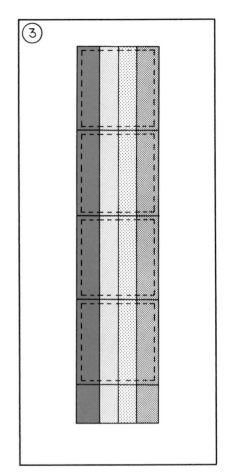

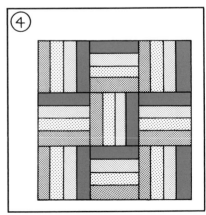

TEMPLATES

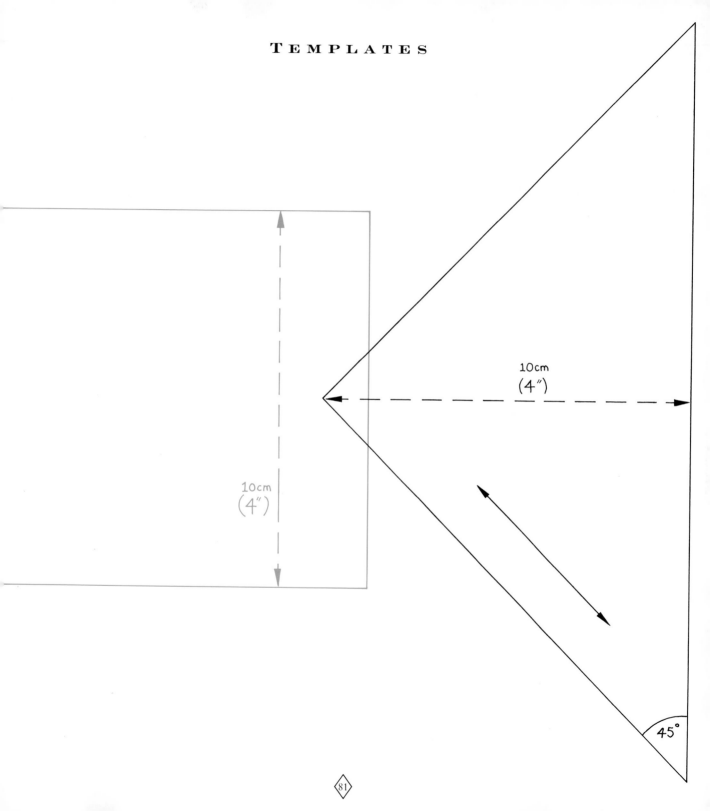

10cm
(4")

10cm
(4")

45°

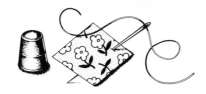

BASKET OF GRAPES

Templates are given for the grapes, leaves and
basket, but the actual arrangement is yours. The inspiration
for this design was the printed panels of the 1810s.
Here the design has been made into a picture, but it could
equally well form the centre of a framed quilt.

REQUIREMENTS

50 cm (½ yard) dress weight
  fabric for foundation fabric (this
  is part of design, so choose the
  colour carefully)
Small pieces of dress weight
  cotton fabrics in green for
  leaves and stalk, mauve and
  purple shades for grapes
1 piece of fabric, 15 × 25 cm (6
  × 10 in) for basket backing
25 cm (¼ yard) dress weight
  cotton for basket 'weave'
  (made from bias strips)
A4 (8¼ × 11⅝ in) sheet of white
  card (use white as the fabrics
  are ironed over the templates
  and coloured or waxed card
  would stain fabrics)
Sewing threads to match fabrics
  to be applied
Very small amount of wadding
Stranded cotton embroidery
  threads for detailing

CONSTRUCTION

When sewing appliqué into natural
shapes, do not worry if the shapes
are not exactly the same as the
templates, in this case the templates
are guides and artistic interpretation
reigns! Use a very small stitch,
angling it under the edge of the
seam allowance, so that it is nearly

①

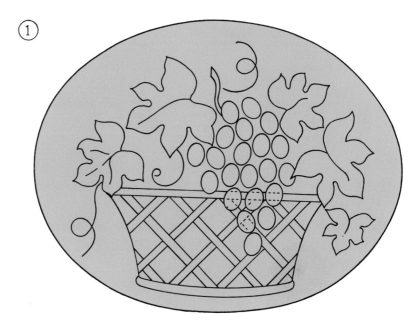

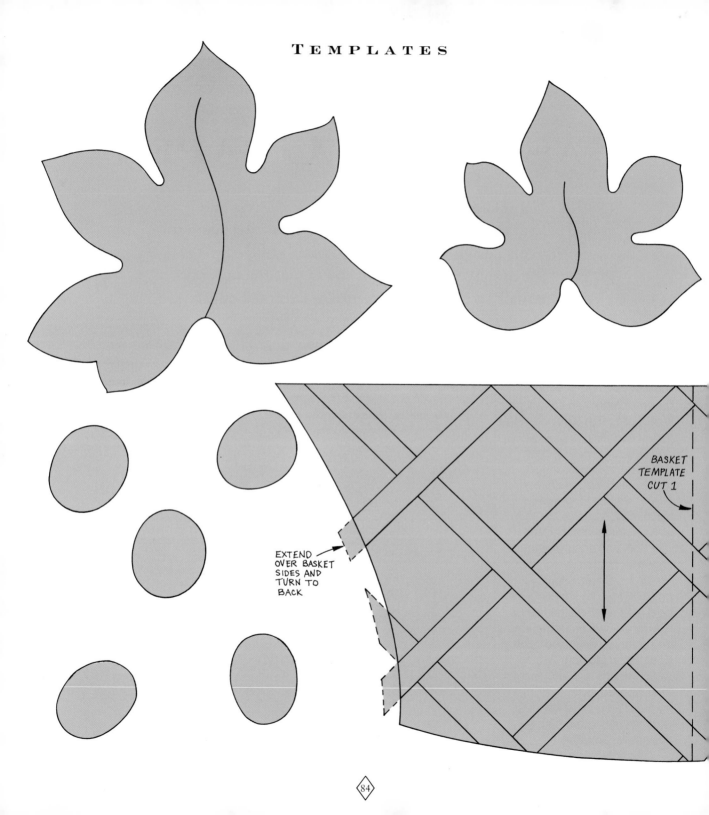

EXTEND
OVER BASKET
SIDES AND
TURN TO
BACK

BASKET
TEMPLATE
CUT 1

invisible. Match the sewing threads carefully to the fabric being applied.

Trace the leaf shapes on to tracing paper and glue lightly to the white card with a glue stick. Cut with paper scissors.

Cut the template for the basket backing by folding the tracing paper in half and matching the dotted line to the fold line. Cut, then transfer the shape to the white card.

Cut three or four different grape shapes in thin white card.

Using the templates, draw the design on to the foundation fabric in a light coloured pencil. Diagram 1 shows the positioning.

Reverse the leaf shapes, place on the wrong side of the fabric, and mark around them carefully, adding 6 mm (¼ in) seam allowance.

Clip into the inner curves almost to the stitching line and snip occasionally around the leaf (diagram 2). Leaving the template in place, fold the seam allowance back

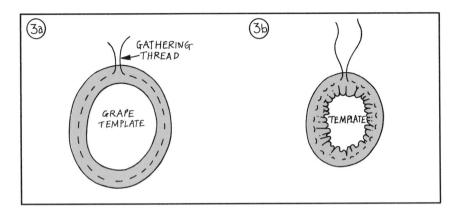

over the template. Press with the tip of the iron, having slightly dampened the seam allowance with a little spray starch. (Spray starch into a saucer and use fingers.)

When dry, remove the template and trim the seam allowances a little but do not cut off the 'tails' that will

form on the leaf corners. The leaf shape will look a little odd at this stage but will be improved when it is sewn in position, as the sewing needle is used to mould the shape.

Cut 21 grape shapes from the mauve and purple fabrics, using the different card templates and adding

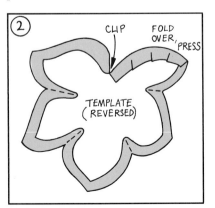

6 mm (¼ in) seam allowance. With a small running stitch, sew a gathering thread inside the seam allowance (diagram 3a). Place the templates in the centre, pull up the gathering thread, then press with the tip of the iron and remove the template when cool (diagram 3b).

Cut out one basket backing with 6 mm (¼ in) seam allowance. Turn in the seam allowance on the sides of the basket only, tack. Mark the position of the diagonal basket 'weave'.

Cut ten strips of fabric on the true bias (at a 45° angle across the fabric). Each strip should be about 25 cm (10 in) long and 3 cm (1¼ in) wide. Fold the strips in half lengthwise, *wrong sides together*, and stitch together, leaving 3 mm (⅛ in) seam allowance. Do not turn the strip through, it will be stitched down on both edges with the seam hidden underneath. Iron the strips so that the seam is in the centre (diagram 4). (Metal gauges can be bought from some suppliers, the fabrics are then ironed with the gauge inside, giving a uniformly even strip.)

Tack these strips on to the basket backing, with the seam underneath, lining them up with the diagonal markings and weaving at the junctions. Fold the ends over the basket sides, but trim level with the raw edge at the top and base of the basket. Stitch in place along both edges.

Tack the basket shape in position on

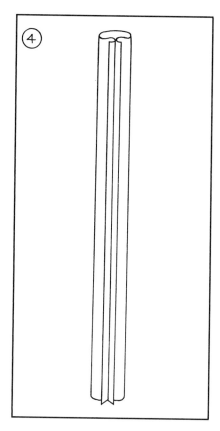

the foundation fabric. Stitch the sides, then finish the basket by covering the top and base lines with two bias strips, neatening the ends. Remove any visible tacking stitches.

Sew the leaves in place with small, neat stitches, tucking in the excess fabric, which appears on the leaf points. On the inside curves, mould the line with the needle point and stitch with a series of tight, small oversewing stitches to strengthen this potentially weak area.

To make the stem, cut a bias strip of fabric 25 mm (1 in) wide. Turn one

short end in, then fold in half lengthwise, place in position on the foundation fabric, and stitch along the side of the stem, through all layers, with small running stitches and with the folded end at the top of the stalk (diagram 5a). Trim away excess seam allowance and roll the folded edge of the strip over the seam allowance (diagram 5b).

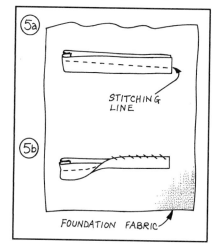

STITCHING LINE

FOUNDATION FABRIC

Stitch, moulding the fabric to the stem shape, leaving the bottom a little longer than the finished stem. It will be covered by a grape.

Place a little teased out wadding inside each grape. Pin in position and stitch around each shape. Embroider the veins on the leaves and tendrils with two strands of cotton, using stem stitch.

The work photographed was framed professionally: backed with wadding and placed in a double mount.

Preparation

Complete the patchwork top including any borders that might be required, then press gently.

Fold the backing, which should be 5 cm (2 in) larger than the top fabric, into quarters and mark the centre top, sides and bottom with glass-headed pins. Lay out flat and tape or pin down, wrong side uppermost.

Fold the wadding into quarters and lay on top of the backing in top left hand quarter, lining up the folds with the marker pins on the backing. Open out carefully on to the backing.

Fold the patchwork into quarters and mark the centres as before with glass-headed pins. Lay on the top left quarter of the wadding over the backing fabric, matching the marker pins. Open out carefully. Pin all the layers together, starting from the centre, smoothing the fabric gently to outer edges (diagram 1).

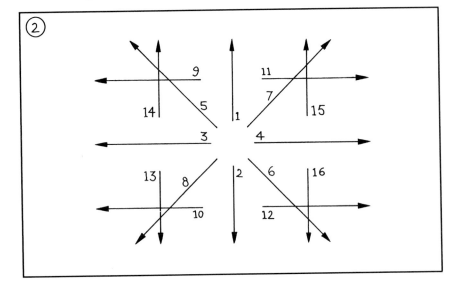

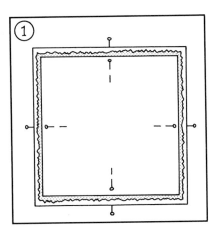

Tacking

Tacking is the key to successful, non-wrinkled quilting. Tack very thoroughly for even the smallest project – this is boring but very necessary. Use straight tacking stitches in the sequence shown in diagram 2. You should finish with a tacked grid in which the distance between any two lines of tacking is not more than 7.5 cm (3 in), regardless of the size of the project.

Frames

A frame is not essential. However, a large round hoop can be used to quilt items as large as a bed covering. Once the 'sandwich' has been securely tacked, place the inner ring of the hoop under the centre of the quilt. When the upper ring is placed in position, there should be a little give in the textile to allow for manipulation while

quilting. Always remove the top ring after each session of quilting. Continue moving the hoop away from the centre. Smaller items can be quilted in a needlepoint frame.

Quilting stitch

Cut a length of thread no longer than 45 cm (18 in), knot one end and run the thread across beeswax.

Run the needle through the top fabric and wadding only, 25 mm (1 in) or so away from where you will begin. Bring the needle up at the required starting point, 'pop' the knot through the top.

Sew with even stitches. Each stitch must penetrate all three layers and the length of the stitch and the gap between should be about the same.

To finish off the thread, make a knot, slide the needle along through the top into the wadding and up through the top, 'popping' the knot through into the wadding. Cut the thread close to the fabric.

N.B. It has been stressed that quilting is a running stitch. However, when quilting patchwork and appliqué it may be necessary to make an occasional stab stitch (page 92) where seams meet, because of the extra layers of fabric caused by seam allowances.

Quilting in the ditch

When stitching the patchwork top together, press the seam allowances the same way (wherever possible on to the darker fabric), then quilt as close as possible to the seam line

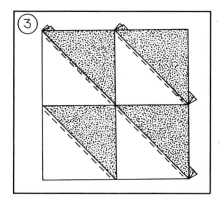

through the single top fabric, wadding and backing (diagram 3).

Outline quilting

It is important when *cutting* the patches that all the seam allowances

are cut accurately to 6 mm (¼ in). When quilting it is then possible to outline the shape 6 mm (¼ in) in from the seams, avoiding unnecessary layers of fabric (diagram 4).

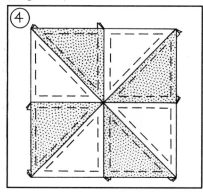

FINISHING

The edges of a patchwork can be finished in a number of ways:

1. Fold the patchwork top seam allowance over the trimmed wadding, then turn the backing seam allowance inwards also. Sew two rows of running stitches

through all the layers, one row very near the edge, the other row about 1 cm (½ in) in from the edge (diagram 1).

2. Bring the backing over to the front to create a border (or vice versa). To do this, trim the top and

wadding to the required finished size, this is then the fold line for the backing. Bring the backing over on to the patchwork top. (Bring over at least 1 cm/½ in.) Turn in the raw edge and slip stitch or quilt through all the layers, mitring the corners (diagram 2).

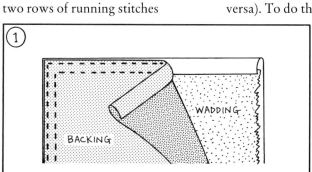

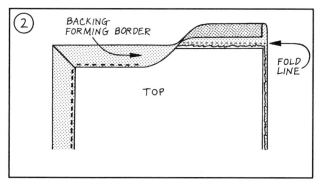

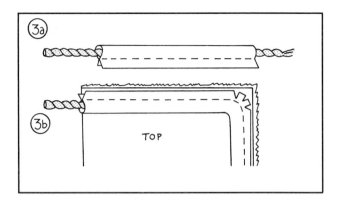

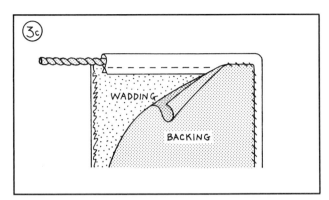

3. Make a piped edge. To do this, cover the piping cord with a bias strip, having first boiled the piping cord to shrink it, if it is not pre-shrunk (diagram 3a). Tack the covered cord to the right side of the patchwork, through the patchwork top and wadding only (diagram 3b). Turn the raw edges in, thus bringing the piped cord to the edge of the patchwork. Trim the backing if necessary and slip stitch into place (diagram 3c).

4. Bind the edges. To do this, cut a bias strip six times the desired finished width. Fold the strip in half, matching long edges and use doubled. This double thickness binding gives a full, rounded edge which will wear well. Single binding which will need a seam allowance on both sides can also be used. This will be four times the finished width.

Stitch in position through all the layers, i.e. through both thicknesses of binding, patchwork top, wadding and backing.

To mitre the corners, pin the bias strip in place, stitch along the seam line of the patchwork only, *not* into the seam allowance. Finish the thread securely. Insert a pin at a 45° angle to the corner (diagram 4a). Fold the strip back over the pin (diagram 4b), then fold the strip down along the second edge. Pin and stitch along the stitching line

only to the next corner, then proceed as above (diagram 4c).

Fold the bias strip at the top edge over on to the backing, slip stitch into place, then crease the fold on the corner.

Fold the bias strip over the second edge, thus making a neat mitre (diagram 4d). Slip stitch in place.

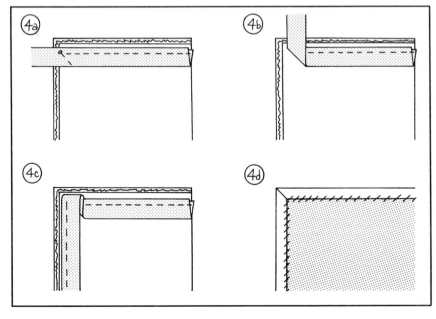

CARE AND CONSERVATION

CARING FOR TEXTILES

Sunlight is the main enemy of textiles, it fades and rots the fabrics, so try to protect them from direct sunlight. Dust and dirt also cause problems.

Air the quilts from time to time, on a breezy, fresh day by hanging them over a clothes line which has been padded with a sheet. Lay the quilt over the line right sides down to protect from sunlight. Shake the quilt well from time to time, leave for about an hour. This will freshen the textile and allow dust to be removed. Where it is not possible to air a quilt, use a vacuum cleaner set at minimum suction. Cover the nozzle with a piece of muslin (firmly secured) and clean gently.

STORAGE

Rolling – if a quilt has to be stored, rolling is the best method. Use a tube (from inside furnishing fabrics) and wrap this with wadding. Lay acid-free tissue paper over the quilt surface, then roll the quilt on to the tube, right side out. Slide the roll into a cotton bag.

This obviously makes a rather long 'parcel', but this method should be used with silk, as folding can crack the textile.

Folding – it may be necessary to fold a quilt: to avoid sharp creases, lay acid-free tissue paper over the quilt and lay wadding where fold lines will occur. Fold carefully, then place in a large cotton bag or fold in a sheet. Do not stack other items on top as this will increase pressure on the folds.

Do not use plastic bags or plastic sheeting to store textiles. They attract dirt and will encourage mould.

CLEANING

Silk and wool quilts or coverlets are usually better professionally dry cleaned.

Most cotton quilts can be washed, but test for colourfastness and note that quilts with cotton wadding can become lumpy and are extremely heavy when wet.

Cotton quilts with polyester wadding can usually be washed by hand on a breezy, fresh day. For larger items it will be necessary to wash in the bath, in cool water with good quality soap flakes. Squeeze out as much of the excess water as possible (do not wring, but a short spin can be used if the article will fit into a machine). Hang, right side underneath, on a clothes line which has been padded with a sheet. Shake frequently during drying time. (If possible get help to take the quilt from the bath to the line.)

When dry, the quilt can be steamed. Using a steam iron, pass the iron over the quilt *without actually letting the weight of the iron down on to the quilt.* The heat of the iron would flatten polyester wadding and it *would not recover.*

CLEANING ANTIQUE QUILTS

Be very careful, take expert advice.

OLD QUILTS AND PATCHWORK FRAGMENTS

These items are sometimes very worn, so think carefully whether they appeal to you, if they do, and the price is reasonable, then buy and enjoy them. Many mosaic fragments are offered for sale, sometimes with the papers still in place. Here, although unused, some of the silks can have rotted. However, if the overall design and colour is appealing the patchwork can be conserved by covering with fine silk net.

GLOSSARY

'American' or seamed method A method of constructing patchwork in which patches are stitched together by hand or machine using a seam.

Appliqué Sewing fabric shapes onto a background fabric by hand or machine.

Appliqué Perse Cutting out printed motifs and applying them to a background fabric.

Bias strip A strip cut diagonally across the warp and weft threads of a piece of fabric.

Block A complete unit of a patchwork design.

Butter muslin/Cheesecloth Used with carded sheep's wool for *wadding*.

Card/Cardboard or Lightweight illustration board Used for *templates*.

Cartridge paper/Drawing paper Used for backing papers for the *'English'* method of patchwork.

Celtic appliqué Bias strips of fabric applied in intricate, interlocking, curved designs.

Domette/Flannelette A fabric used for padding.

'English' or paper method A method of constructing patchwork in which paper shapes are cut from a template, the fabrics are then cut with seam allowances and tacked over the papers. These are then *oversewn* together on the wrong side.

Grain line A line following the warp threads, i.e. parallel to the selvage of the fabric.

Ladder stitch Worked by hand. This is an invisible method of stitching two edges together. Fold the seam allowances to the wrong side and place the two shapes next to one another right side up and with the folds adjacent. Slide the needle along the folded edge of one shape for a short distance bringing it out on the edge, then insert the needle into the folded edge of the second shape exactly opposite. Slide along the fold and so on. The stitching can be pulled tight at the end of the seam before finishing off.

Marked line Line drawn round a template marking the stitching line.

Mosaic patchwork Intricate linking of patchwork shapes, often constructed using papers.

Oversewing/Overcasting An embroidery stitch used to bind an edge.

Patchwork The construction of a complete new textile using shaped patches stitched together using *'American'* or *'English'* methods.

Piping cord/Filler cord Strong cord available in various diameters, which is encased in fabric to make a decorative edging.

Polystyrene/Styrofoam A lightweight board suitable for pinning patchwork shapes onto.

Press studs/Snaps Used for fastening two pieces of fabric together.

Quilting The stitching together of a three layered sandwich of textiles: top, *wadding* and backing, using running stitches.

Sashing or setting strips/Dividers Lattice strips of fabric which are used to divide or outline the *blocks* when assembling them into a complete top.

Set square/Right-angled triangle Useful when constructing templates.

Slip stitch Worked by hand. Slide the needle along the fold of the fabric for a short distance, then take up a small amount of the backing fabric and take the needle back into the fold, ensuring that the stitches are almost invisible.

Stab stitch Worked by hand. Keep the needle at 90° to the work, take the needle through all layers to the back of the work, then push the needle back, again at 90°, through to the front and so on. This enables small, tight stitches to be made through many layers of fabric.

Stay stitching Worked by hand or machine. A continuous line of stitching through a single layer of fabric to give strength.

Tack, tacking/Baste, basting A large, temporary running stitch.

Template The exact pattern from which patchwork fabric or paper shapes will be cut.

Wadding/Batting The middle, soft and fluffy layer of the quilt sandwich, which gives it warmth and loft.

ACKNOWLEDGEMENTS

Picture framing by Ian Hunter.

Crib hand carved by Phyllis Branston.

Roman Stripe quilt by Paula Walmsley.

Double Wedding Ring quilt in progress by Mary Atkins.

INDEX

Acrilan wadding 14
Album quilts 13
American method 20
Antique quilts 11–13, 91
Appliqué 11–13, 18, 83–87
Assembling blocks 52

Barn raising 64, 69
Bear's paw 53
Beeswax 15
Betweens needles 14
Block designs 17, 51–69
Borders 52

Card 15
Carded sheep's wool 14
Caring for textiles 91
Castle wall 50, 51, 53, 62–63
Choosing fabric 16
Christmas projects 27, 30–33, 34–37, 38–41, 42–45
Classic wadding 14
Cleaning 91
Cleaning antique quilts 91
Colour scheme 16
Construction, method of 20
Cork tile 15
Corner stones 69
Cotton 14
Cotton wadding 14
Courthouse steps 69

Crazy patchwork 12, 18
Crewel needles 14
Curved seam patchwork 18, 71
Cutting fabrics 19
Cutting mat 15
Cutting templates 19

Design plan 16
Design sheet 53, 69
Domette 14
Double wedding ring 51, 70–75
Double wrench 53
Drafting 18, 51
Drawing paper 15
Drawing templates 18

Eight-pointed star 18, 53
English method 21, 23

Fabrics 14, 16
Finishing 89–90
Flower basket 53
Foundation square 68
Frames 88
Friendship quilts 13

Graph paper 15

Hand sewing 21
Hawaiian quilts 12, 13

Hexagon-based designs 17

Light and dark 65, 69
Log cabin 51, 64–69

Making templates 19
Mosaic patchwork 12

Needles, hand sewing 14
Needles, machine sewing 14

Outline quilting 89

Papers 15
Patchwork, history 11–13
Pencils 15
Pins 14
Planning sheets 54–55
Plastic sheet 15
Polyester cotton blends 14
Polyester wadding 14
Polystyrene tile 15
Preparation (quilting) 88

Queen Charlotte's crown 51, 53, 56–57
Quilting 11–13, 88–89
Quilt in the ditch 89
Quilting stitch 88

Rail fence 80
Roman stripes 80
Rotary cutter 15

Ruler 15

Sandpaper 15
Scissors 15
Seamed patchwork 20
Seminole 13, 76–79
Sewing machine 15, 21
Sewing thread 15
Sharps needles 14
Silk 14
Silk wadding 14
St Louis star 51, 53, 60–61
Star within a star 53
Storage 91
Straight furrow 69
Strip patchwork 76, 80–81
Strip templates 15

Tacking (quilting) 88
Templates 15, 18, 19
Thick & thin strips 69
Thimble 15

Variable star 51, 53, 58–59

Wadding 14
Washing fabrics 16
Windmill 53
Window templates 19
Wool 14
Woollen blankets 14

PRINTED IN BELGIUM BY

proost
INTERNATIONAL BOOK PRODUCTION